**Canada in the Atlantic Economy**

# CANADA IN THE ATLANTIC ECONOMY

**Published:**

# Canada in a Wider Economic Community

H. Edward English, Bruce W. Wilkinson, H. C. Eastman

Published for the
Private Planning Association of Canada by University of Toronto Press

# To William B. Lambert

These studies of "Canada in the Atlantic Economy" are dedicated with respect and gratitude to the late William B. Lambert, Chairman of the Board of the Private Planning Association of Canada from 1965 to 1967, who played a vital role in the development and supervision of the Atlantic Economic Studies Program, on which the publications are based.

His interest went far beyond his formal responsibility; he held a deep conviction concerning the importance of international cooperation among the North Atlantic nations. His untimely death came when the first draft studies had entered the early stages of publication.

© University of Toronto Press 1972 / Toronto and Buffalo / Reprinted 2017 / ISBN 978-0-8020-3305-5 (paper)/ Microfiche ISBN 0-8020-0334-6

# Foreword

There have been two outstanding developments in international trade policy during the past twenty years—the multilateral dismantling of trade barriers under the General Agreement on Tariffs and Trade, which has been the agency for several rounds of successful tariff negotiations since its inception in 1947, and the etablishment of the European Economic Community and the European Free Trade Association in the late 1950s. In a period of reconstruction and then sustained growth, these policies have helped the participating nations of the Atlantic area to experience the benefits of international specialization and expanding trade. The wealth generated by trade and domestic prosperity has also made possible external aid programs to assist economic growth in the developing countries.

Whatever the trade and economic development problems of the future, it is widely acknowledged that the industrially advanced countries of the North Atlantic region must play an important role. It is also generally conceded that the ability of these countries to maintain their own economic growth and prosperity and to contribute to that of the less advanced nations will be greatly enhanced if they can reduce or remove the remaining trade barriers among themselves. Cooperation among Atlantic countries is now fostered by the GATT and by the Organisation for Economic Co-operation and Development. But the success of these and other approaches depends on the assessment by each country of the importance of international trade liberalization and policy coordination for its domestic economy and other national interests. This is particularly true for countries such as Canada which are heavily dependent upon export markets.

The Atlantic Economic Studies Program of the Private Planning Association of Canada was initiated to study the implications for Canada of trade liberalization and closer economic integration among the nations bordering the North Atlantic. It is planned to issue some fourteen paperbound volumes, incorporating over twenty studies by leading Canadian and foreign economists. Despite the technical nature of much of the subject matter, the studies have been written in language designed to appeal to the non-professional reader.

The directors and staff of the Private Planning Association wish to acknowledge the financial support which made this project possible—a grant from the Ford Foundation and the contributions of members of the Association. They are also appreciative of the help that has been provided by very many individuals in the preparation and review of all the studies—in discussions and correspondence with authors, at the Association's November, 1966, conference on "Canada and the Atlantic Economy," and on other occasions.

H. E. ENGLISH
Director of Research
Atlantic Economic Studies Program

# Preface to the Concluding Volume

With the issue of this final volume in the series *Canada in the Atlantic Economy*, this publication venture comes to a conclusion. The occasion provides an appropriate opportunity to extend thanks to all who have co-operated in the realization of the aims of this project.

The project has been sponsored by the Private Planning Association of Canada and financed jointly by the Association and the Ford Foundation, which provided a grant of $180,000 in support of the research program. It has been a completely independent project. The terms of reference were re-viewed by a small steering committee at the outset, but the subsequent work has been the responsibility of the individual authors and of the Director and Associate Director of Research. The staff of the Private Planning Association have helped the research directors in editing and in determining the publish-ability of each manuscript. In those instances where studies did not reach publication, a variety of considerations affected the decision, but in all cases the researcher has concurred in the decision. Delays in the publication of individual studies and, consequently, in the completion of the summary volume may be attributed in part to that malaise of the economist, excess demand for his services, and to the tendency—or perhaps temptation—of economists (like some other professionals) to be drawn into administrative activity, inside and outside universities.

Fortunately, the timeliness of some policy issues does not soon fade. This appears to apply especially strongly to commercial-policy questions in Canada. The Atlantic Studies Program was motivated by Canadian concern over the consequences of European regionalism for Canada's trade and other economic relations with Europe and the United States. That was in the mid-1960s. Today, in 1972, the same concern prevails. Some circumstances have changed—the British application to join the European Economic Com-munity has been accepted, the Kennedy Round tariff cuts have been effected, Japan has entered more strongly into the calculations of Atlantic "partners," exchange rates have been adjusted. But the fundamental issue for Canada remains very substantially what it was in 1965—how to live as a relatively smaller economic unit in a world where nearly all of the developed nations are participating in huge free-trading blocs encompassing markets of one hundred million persons or more.

The *Canada in the Atlantic Economy* series does not provide a conclusive answer to this question. What it does hope to do is to enlarge the body of information available on the implications of substantial commercial-policy changes for Canada and to stimulate the thinking of policy-makers and others on the merits and limitations of the wider range of policy options that now appear relevant to Canada's economic and political interests.

While there has been considerable discussion between the authors of the interrelationships among chapters of this study and of the content of individual chapters, the major responsibility for the eight chapters may be assigned as follows: Chapters 2, 3, and 4, Bruce W. Wilkinson; Chapter 7, Harry C. Eastman; and the remainder, H. Edward English. In Chapter 5, E. M. Cape assisted substantially in the summarizing of the individual industry studies.

H. Edward English
Director of Research

# Contents

# 1. Introduction

Canada is an outward-looking country. The reasons are deeply imbedded in Canadian history, geography, and economics. Long periods of colonial association, first with France and then with Britain, established Canada's cultural and political traditions. The proximity and ready access to the United States of over 90 percent of Canadian settlement have ensured modern Canada of close ties and common attitudes with its great neighbour. But perhaps above all, Canada's great natural wealth has, in effect, denied it any possibility of an autarkic existence. The wealth of farm, forest, and mine vastly exceeds Canada's current or foreseeable domestic needs, and the income earned through the export of these products has long been the source for financing imports of capital goods to build the Canadian economy and consumer goods that give substance to a high standard of living.

Most Canadians take these international relations for granted. They never stop to contemplate a situation in which opportunities to benefit from trade and other foreign commerce would not exist. It is ironic that a few Canadian nationalists would have Canada attempt to extinguish its dependence on trade with the United States, thus fostering attitudes that are more common in that country, with its capacity for a much higher degree of self-sufficiency. Fortunately, such a convergence with American attitudes is impossible, since Canadians would never accept the loss of spending power that a serious effort at self-sufficiency would impose.

Yet to acknowledge that interdependence is essential to Canada's high living standard is not to deny the existence of a problem. Since Canada's political independence is in the final analysis guaranteed by U.S. military strength, the country's major international challenges relate mainly to its economic relationships. Canada is a substantial *economic* power, while perhaps only once in its history—for a few years at the end of World War II—has it been a significant *political* power. Canada's influence, on behalf of its own interests and of those of other nations, is strongly felt where world trade and investment are concerned. The Canadian share of world trade greatly exceeds the country's ranking by any of the usual military or political criteria. It is the most important trading partner of the United States and the recipient of more private U.S. investment than any other country. This position gives Canada a role in international trade negotiations and in the making of rules affecting international capital flows that exerts a real impact on the United States and on the chief trading partners of both countries. How has Canada used its influence in the international economic-policy arena, and what opportunities exist today?

Canada's trade and investment policies have always been dominated by the needs of national development. For most of the first century of Canadian history the three main factors of these policies were:

(a) the use of protective policies, especially the so-called National Policy dating from 1879, as an inducement to the establishment of secondary industry;

(b) the maintenance of preferential access to the British market;

(c) the search for an optimum degree of interdependence with the United States.

Contradiction is, of course, inherent in the simultaneous search for these policy goals, but a workable if somewhat short-sighted compromise had evolved during the first third of this century. British "free trade" and imperial policy permitted the dominions to impose much higher trade barriers against imports from the United Kingdom than Britain imposed upon imports from them. As for the Canada-U.S. relationship, a more awkward compromise, achieved through the structure of the import tariff, permitted Canada ready access to U.S. capital goods, while Canadian consumer-goods manufacturers were able to enjoy high levels of effective protection. Also, a liberal Canadian policy towards foreign investment ensured first British and later American investors ample opportunity to produce in Canada without fear of effective import competition—or indeed, in the small domestic market, of much internal competition.

The 1930s saw the erosion of this somewhat difficult but reasonably viable pattern of policy. To an important degree, circumstances affecting all three of the elements noted above had changed and were about to change still further. Britain had already abandoned free trade under the pressure of unemployment caused by the overvaluation of the pound in the 1920s and the gradual loss of its industrial supremacy. Canada-U.S. trade had fallen victim to the defensive protection of the depression. While the Ottawa agreements preserved important features of Canada's unilateral preferred access to the British market, their immediate purpose was to stop imports from the United States in the interest of preserving a larger share of the depressed home market for Canadian manufacturers.

The war brought additional changes in the circumstances affecting Canada's trade. Not only was Britain's relative position further weakened, but

Canadian manufacturing industry was greatly stimulated. With the steady growth in Canada's population and per capita income, the domestic market in the early postwar years had become a much improved base for many manufacturing activities. Finally, the chaos that had beset international trade during the 1930s generated a will to organize postwar trading relationships on a more orderly and more liberal basis.

As peace dawned, Canada found itself in harness with the United States, leading the forces for multilateral trade liberalization and monetary stabilization. By the end of the 1950s the reconstruction of Europe made it possible for all North Atlantic countries to experience the benefits of a freer flow of goods and reasonably stable currencies.

However, European reconstruction also introduced a new force in international trade relationships—the regional common market. The European Economic Community was essentially a means by which a group of developed countries sought to go beyond the trade liberalization possible in the multilateral context provided by the General Agreement on Tariffs and Trade (GATT). The motivation, especially in the early stages, was largely political—the hope that in functional integration the countries of war-torn Europe could find a basis for unity as well as for reconstruction—and because of this the European phenomenon may have been unique. For this reason also, the movement for Europe's integration risked a loss of enthusiasm once the imperatives of the early postwar years faded away with restored political stability and economic health in the European countries. But in spite of the reassertion of nationalism, especially in the French government, the European Economic Community has survived. While considerable momentum has been lost, the EEC has demonstrated that its vitality is based on realized benefits to economic groups that represent durable forces for political cooperation on the European continent. For the French farmer and German and Italian manufacturers, as well as for a large share of the working population, the operation of the Community has become inextricably associated with a rising standard of living. More than that, an important part of the intellectual leadership of Europe—and particularly that of the younger generation—finds its identity more in Europe than in its component parts. Myths of European personality are being erected on the more earthy reality of converging consumption patterns.

The social dynamism of Western Europe has had important consequences for other countries all around the world. Most important, for the Eastern European bloc of Communist countries it has given convincing evidence that Western liberalism would not crumble away in favour of Marxist Communism. Thus, these events have played a major role in replacing the Cold War with a new era of determined, if not so far very productive, negotiation.

The post-1950 developments have also transformed the relationships of all European countries with the United States. The postwar years—and particularly the past decade—have seen the role of dependency gradually replaced by a confident indifference to American affairs, though European attitudes stop well short of any general willingness to have U.S. forces withdrawn from European soil or the nuclear deterrent modified. Part of the changed relationship has been associated with U.S. preoccupation with Southeast Asia and with domestic social and racial unrest—problems for which Europe feels little interest or sympathy. This indifference has also brought a reaction in the United States, mainly against Europe's lack of support for the Asian version of the fight against Communism. Many Europeans point out that the United States was all too willing to see an expeditious withdrawal of European colonial powers from Asia (and later from Africa). Why should they now return on conditions established by uncertain American administrations since the mid-1950s?

The attitudes born of this separation of interests have not seriously affected economic relations across the Atlantic. Basically prosperous economies have demonstrated the scope and the vitality of world trade and international business, and neither alarums of "le défi américain" nor U.S. controls on capital outflows have much slowed the evolution towards both common consumption standards and increasingly overlapping corporate "families."

There is an awareness—made more acute by unilateral measures taken by the United States in the summer and fall of 1971—that economic relationships cannot be taken for granted, that important trade barriers remain, and that a wide variety of non-tariff barriers may rise to fill the role vacated by the prohibitive import tariffs of the past. The operations of interventionist governments have distorted trade patterns, and increased intra-corporate transfers of intermediate goods have obscured the significance of traditional methods for classifying and valuing trade flows. But perhaps the most direct challenges to the continuity of economic relationships lie in agricultural protectionism, on the one hand, and unwillingness by both Europe and the United States to face up to the implications of rising manufactured exports from Asia—that is, from both Japan and the Far Eastern developing countries—on the other. Lip service has been paid to the idea of tariff preferences, but the true measures of American and European policy are the long-term cotton textile agreement and those euphemistically "voluntary" export restraints. Every country defends these devices on grounds that they are the least bad among alternatives, but none seeks a cooperative route to more liberal policies with any real enthusiasm.

Although in the early 1970s it is the U.S. Congress that is pictured as beating a retreat from liberal trade principles, in fact on both agricultural protection and so-called low-wage imports it is Europe that has adopted the more restrictive policies. Even the arrangements giving preferential access to European markets for products of the EEC's Associated Overseas Territories have really provided substantial scope only for the exports of tropical products. Since African countries are not likely, in the near future, to be important exporters of those manufactures not uniquely based on tropical resources, Europe has been able, by concentrating on Africa's needs, largely to avoid this challenge from Asian competition. Japan's own record of selective protectionism has made it easy for Europe to rationalize a restrictive view towards Japan's manufactured exports, and it is therefore in a North American-Japanese confrontation that this problem has come to the fore.

The main challenge to trade policy in the 1970s is symptomized by the two issues mentioned in the foregoing paragraph:

1. The conflict between those who, as efficient or potentially efficient producers of the products of extensive agriculture, are anxious to exploit the opportunity for agricultural specialization and those who believe that they can and should be self-reliant, if not entirely self-sufficient, in food. The United States, Canada, and Australia are ranged against the EEC and (separately and to a lesser extent) Japan in this matter.

2. The conflict between efficient producers of so-called labour-intensive manufactures and countries attempting to produce competing goods under higher wage conditions. In this debate it is the United States (and, to a lesser extent, Canada) that is arrayed against Japan and the rising developing countries of Asia, while Western Europe stands largely aloof with a policy that is already restrictive towards imports of such products.

*The future of the Atlantic community*

What role has the Atlantic community—or, less pretentiously, the Atlantic trading countries as a group—to play in the resolution of these conflicts? More specifically:

1. What can be done through established negotiation mechanisms such as GATT or consultative bodies such as the OECD? What about the prospects for progress through UNCTAD?

2. Is some new approach possible—for example, regional cooperation either among Atlantic or Pacific countries or among some of these nations in conjunction with certain developing countries? Can the example of regional initiative established by Europe be followed by others in the search for responses to the new economic challenges?

3. Finally, what role can Canada play? Faced by a restored Europe to the

east and a reconstructed and dynamic Japan to the west, is Canada only an interested bystander, occasionally whispering into the American ear as it contends with overseas partners?

To evaluate the significance for Canada of the kind of Atlantic or world economy likely to evolve during the 1970s, it is important to identify the most probable directions of change and locus of challenge or opportunity.

We will first assess the relevance of existing institutions to those who formulate international economic policies. In the first place, there is no fundamental challenge to established postwar international arrangements that have been dominated by the Atlantic nations. Even though they were designed as more universal institutions, GATT and the IMF continue to command the support primarily of the leading trading nations of the non-Communist world. The IMF, as a unique institution in the service of monetary stability, has been adapted reasonably well to changing circumstances. GATT is only now facing a similar need for adaptation. It must try to devise means of liberalizing trade restrictions that do not take the readily measurable form of tariffs. In particular, it must contend with agricultural and other non-tariff barriers that are deeply rooted in national policies that often have a developmental or redistributive purpose. The functions of these devices thus go far beyond the revenue-gathering or limited protective purpose of a duty on imports, which modifies but never denies the allocation role of the market. Can negotiations in a multilateral context ever adequately cover the enormous variety of devices that fall in the negative classification of non-tariff barriers? The answer is as yet unknown, but it appears really to depend on how much is expected of GATT in the future. If it is expected to act as the conscience of the world's traders, always reminding them how national practices or bilateral arrangements conflict with its non-discriminatory principles, then its role is secure. But if further substantial moves towards liberalization of trade are desired, the likelihood that they can come through GATT is more doubtful.

Possibly one of the more promising areas for a contribution by the GATT secretariat may be in developing guidelines for expanding trade between the market-oriented and centrally planned economies. However, for the other set of important trade relationships—that between developed and developing countries—GATT seems ill-equipped, at least for the present, given the limited direct representation of developing countries among its signatories. Notwithstanding the unilateral granting of Kennedy Round concessions to developing countries, the major consequence of these negotiations was clearly the relative neglect of trade liberalization for the type of manufactures of which such countries are, or hope to be, competitive suppliers.

It is at present difficult to see how any established institution can be employed to effect truly liberal trade policies towards the less developed nations. The UNCTAD, which was basically the invention of the developing countries, has generated many words but little action on their behalf. It is simply too large to be more than a forum, and as such it has afforded opportunity for the scoring of publicity points by contending members of both the developed and the less developed world.

The main alternative to truly multilateral moves towards liberalization of trade, as well as towards reduced incidence of other restrictions to international movement of goods and productive factors, is the regional economic arrangement. For every regional group the one fundamental question arises: Will it be sufficiently outward-looking to avoid the undesirable implications of a trading bloc? No comprehensive answer can be given to such a question, but a few observations are possible.

A trading bloc is more likely to be conducive to trade liberalization if it encompasses a large market area. It is also less likely to have serious trade-diversion effects if it adopts a relatively low external tariff. The evidence on existing regional groups is mixed. The major cases, the EEC and EFTA, both encompass a vast market, and neither has clung to a restrictive policy vis-à-vis non-members except in temperate-zone agricultural products and labour-intensive manufactures. By and large, the most successful regional groups in the developing world have been small—for example, the Central American Common Market and the East African Community. The fact that the smallest countries have the most to gain from economic integration has contributed greatly to the founding of these communities. Since, in all of the groupings listed, no one of the member countries is clearly dominant, the political independence of each member is more easily maintained.

Regional economic groups can be classified by their overall effect as follows:

(a) those in which the benefits to member countries are essentially at the expense of non-members;

(b) those that are practically neutral in impact on non-members;

(c) those actually conducive to the achievement of economic integration and freer trade on a wider scale, either specifically through enlargement of the particular grouping or, more generally, through the demonstration effect, encouraging other countries to do the same.

For most small customs unions, particularly those among developing countries, the effects on non-members are likely to be limited—that is, they fall in the second group. Only small adjacent nations are likely to suffer much from exclusion from this type of customs union, and it is usually not too difficult to admit such countries to the grouping. Among developed countries, the effects are more likely to be significant on outsiders, because such countries have a larger potential for imports. The European Economic Community has a major effect on world trade in agricultural products. At the same time, the strong bargaining position that the EEC acquired for continental Europe generated a much stronger GATT initiative on the part of the United States in what became the Kennedy Round. It is most unlikely that President Kennedy would have put his administration's influence behind the Trade Expansion Act of 1962 if the European grouping had not existed.

The lesson to be learned from this case is that such a grouping is likely to be constructive to the extent that it follows a liberal policy towards non-members. If the founding or dominant member countries use the success of their grouping as a stimulus to others to join—or, at least, to negotiate a reduction in their trade barriers—then a regional group can have a multi-lateral objective.

The proposition that regional grouping can be a good method—perhaps even the best—of moving towards multilateral trade liberalization is strengthened by the nature of the remaining trade barriers described above and by the existence and character of the present European group or groups. For example, the existence of the EFTA has in no way limited the possibility of expansion of the EEC, and because the former group's members were able to develop a consistent position, their association may ease the route for most of them to follow Britain in joining the Community. Similarly, even if Britain had again been rejected as an EEC member, it seems likely that a move to broaden EFTA or to replace it with a larger free trade association would have placed countries outside the Community in a much better bargaining position vis-à-vis the EEC than the more traditional system of negotiation in which each country attempts to bargain individually.

Assuming that most EFTA countries will now succeed in gaining entry to the EEC, what kinds of additional grouping among industrial nations might become relevant? The majority of feasible combinations are variations on one concept: a free trade association open to all nations but having as its initial members the United States and Japan, one or more of Canada, Australia, and New Zealand, and those European countries that cannot, for political reasons, join the European Economic Community as full members. (The latter would be likely to include Switzerland, Sweden, Finland, and Austria.) This concept is defined sufficiently flexibly to be equivalent in effect to any policy for eliminating the major remaining barriers to trade. The concept of an open-ended free trade association is one fairly direct means of realizing the condition required as a basis for the following economic analysis of effects.

The basic political advantage of the larger free trade association over the customs union is that it involves no common external policy. Thus, it permits individual countries to pursue distinctive economic policies with respect to non-members while still giving the more liberal members a chance to take a lead that others might be induced to follow. Countries that seek distinctive political postures, such as neutrality, also apparently distinguish between participation in a free trade association and participation in a customs union, and this distinction has also been accepted implicitly by the Communist countries of Eastern Europe in the case of Finland and Austria.

There can be little doubt that if such a wider association involving all the non-EEC members and observers of the OECD were formed, the EEC would want to negotiate seriously with it.[1] Indeed, if and when the EEC moves on to more complete economic union, as it has expressed its intention of doing, there is no reason why it might not, as a unit, become a member of a larger and less closely knit association. To summarize the basic rationale for such an arrangement, it could embody three purposes:

(1) The achievement of a commitment to eliminate remaining trade obstacles, including the most troublesome non-tariff barriers affecting trade in industrial components and finished goods. In dealing with these problems, an industrial free trade association (as in EFTA) goes well beyond the GATT or UNCTAD in obliging members to examine and remedy those elements of their national policies that are out of keeping with their commitments.

(2) The advancement of more liberal rules governing trade in products of temperate agriculture (including related tropical products). Here there is considerable scope for setting a new example; given the performance of the EEC to date, it is unlikely that a liberal initiative will come from that quarter. Japan's attitude would be of crucial importance to the prospects for designing a liberal policy for agricultural trade.

(3) The offer of unilateral concessions to the developing countries, by reducing not only the trade barriers on tropical products in relatively processed as well as raw forms, but also the barriers affecting the so-called labour-intensive manufactures. The Kennedy Round resulted in helpful concessions on some tropical products, but not in other areas.

With respect to this last point, in Africa, for example, there is a very limited likelihood in the near future of increasing exports of labour-intensive products. But the remainder of the developing world, notably East and South Asia and, increasingly, Latin America, will soon have a capacity for exports of such manufactures. The United States and Japan have a major opportunity

---

[1]Even if the United States and Japan formed a group alone, the same effect might follow, but such an arrangement is most unlikely; the United States would want to participate only if membership were initially larger, and the same would probably apply to Japan.

to expand the market for such exports, but they will be likely to provide this outlet only on a cooperative basis. So long as they act alone, they will tend to fall back on the familiar argument that to give concessions will ruin the domestic industry affected. Furthermore, they will be able and all too willing to point to the restrictive policies of other developed countries.

Thus, cooperative action is essential, and it is much more likely that such action will be taken if, at the same time, the developed countries are expanding their opportunities for trade with one another. A combined free trade association involving the United States, Japan, and others might contemplate significant reduction or elimination of tariffs on textiles and those simpler metal and plastic products that could be competitively supplied today by Korea, Singapore, and India and tomorrow by Indonesia and some of the Latin American countries.

The fact that, in the early 1970s, it is the United States that appears to be retreating from this kind of position is not inconsistent with the foregoing possibilities. It merely emphasizes the need for an American administration to think in terms of a far-reaching initiative, if not a "grand design," in order to continue to play a leading role in international affairs, both economic and political. The idea of a free trade association could fill this role in American policy. But it may not be necessary to go so far. Selective policies for dealing with non-tariff barriers, agricultural trade, or preferential market access for developing-country products may be possible, and cooperation among the United States, Japan, and other OECD countries might be attained through some less ambitious international arrangements. But it is important to stress the need for a policy that makes a substantial contribution to the solution of world economic problems, rather than one that settles for the tokenism characteristic of such schemes as UNCTAD preferences and long-term cotton textile agreements.

In exploring the possibilities for trade policies in the next decade, then, one can see as the main possibilities:

(a) a hold-the-line policy, resisting with varying degrees of success the backsliding tendencies of democratic legislatures under specific protectionist pressure whenever no larger initiatives are being advanced; or

(b) a substantial initiative supported primarily by the United States and Japan, born of the dynamics of Asia and trans-Pacific trade and of the need to fill the current policy vacuum. If, at the start of the decade of the 1970s, such an initiative seems unlikely, it should be remembered that neither of the major economic powers of the Pacific can afford indefinitely a relationship based on Congressional myopia in the one country and administrative restriction in the other. (See p. 145.)

*Canada's role*

The purpose of the present volume is to assess realistically Canada's stake in the Atlantic economy of the last quarter of the twentieth century. It is very easy to conclude in advance that Canada will require no role because no drama is to be staged. But it is well to explore what importance, both economic and political, trade and related policies can have for Canada in the decade ahead. When opportunities for progress towards liberalization of trade arise, it may be too late to consider the implications in any detail. Indeed, it was in the wake of Canada's failure to respond very constructively, even in its own interest, to the Kennedy initiative that the proposal to prepare this series of studies was born.

As has already been suggested, it is well to define the Atlantic community in the OECD sense, to include Japan, Australia, and New Zealand, and to recognize (as the OECD has through its Development Assistance Committee) that the developed countries must relate their efforts at cooperation among themselves to the challenge of development. Furthermore, this is clearly as important in trade policy as in aid programs, although it has not received equal attention until quite recently.

In reviewing Canada's role we will be stressing the significance of closer economic relationships, particularly the integration of the Canadian economy with that of other developed countries through substantial reduction of trade barriers. In line with the foregoing discussion we make the following assumptions:

(*a*)  that Canada is anxious to maintain its political independence, particularly vis-à-vis the United States, and that it will therefore prefer a trade group including other major partners besides the United States; and

(*b*)  that support within Canada for a liberal trade policy depends primarily on the above political consideration, plus assessment of national economic benefits.

An additional assumption should probably be added, which is that Canada is basically committed to maintaining or further liberalizing the present rules governing international trade and that it supports the principles of GATT, the OECD, and UNCTAD. This point is relevant but scarcely imposes a constraint on the following discussion, since it is the implications of further liberalization, and not its rejection, that are being assessed.

On the basis of the stated assumptions, the succeeding chapters of this book focus on an analysis of the effect on the Canadian economy of a substantial reduction of trade barriers among the developed countries, particularly those of the Atlantic region, but with some reference also to the Pacific developed countries. After two brief sections on the historic role of trade in Canadian development, as well as on the character of world trade and the prospects for growth of world markets (Chapters 2 and 3), the main body of this volume deals with the implications for Canada of a wider economic community under the following headings:

Chapter 4, "A First Approximation to Free-Trade Alternatives for Canada," includes an application of measures of the elasticity of trade growth in response to price reductions following the removal of tariff barriers. Some of the more dynamic effects of free trade areas are also reviewed, and distinctions are drawn between the implications of various groupings of developed countries.

Chapter 5, "The Structure of the Canadian Economy," reviews the implications of substantial trade liberalization for selected specific industries as well as for the main regions of Canada. Here an effort is made to indicate the variety of specific effects that might be anticipated from free trade.

Chapter 6, "The Adjustment Mechanism and Its Operation under Trade Liberalization," reviews the implications of the previous findings for the Canadian economy as a whole, focusing particularly on the adjustment mechanism, capital flows, wage levels, and the exchange rate.

Chapter 7, "The Harmonization of Non-Tariff Economic Policies in a Free Trade Area," is an effort to assess areas where harmonization of Canadian public policies with those of trading partners might be most necessary.

Chapter 8, "Some Commercial-Policy Conclusions," reviews the implications of the findings, particularly those in Chapters 4 to 8, for the broader policy issues introduced in the present chapter.

Essentially, however, the purpose of this book is to assess the meaning for Canada of trade liberalization, whatever form it takes. The actual form, whether it is the consequence of an extension of traditional tariff reductions or some bold new initiative designed for the political circumstances of that day, is, so far as economic and domestic political analysis is concerned, secondary. The main question is whether far-reaching trade liberalization is likely to have significant consequences for the rate and pattern of Canadian growth, given the assumption that the political motive is strong enough to promote Canadian participation in any liberalization move or sufficiently weak to prevent Canada from opting out if the initiative is taken by other nations.

# 2. Canadian Trade: Past and Present

Foreign trade has always—from Canada's earliest days—been important to the Canadian economy. Shortly after Confederation, merchandise exports and imports each totaled about 14 percent of gross national product. Today exports are about 20 percent, and imports about 16 percent, of gross national product. The expansion of Canada's foreign trade and the concomitant overall economic development have received intensive analysis in a number of publications.[1] This monograph does not try to survey old ground, nor does it try to delve thoroughly into historical series to attempt some reinterpretation of past events. Rather, the purpose of this chapter is twofold: first, to emphasize several features of the historical growth of Canadian trade and of the domestic economy worth keeping in mind, especially by policy-makers, when assessing the material presented in subsequent chapters on the implications of free trade for Canada; second, to highlight the essential characteristics and determinants of Canadian trade flows in the 1960s.

*A brief historical perspective*

Canadian comparative advantage has traditionally been with natural-resource-based products. The earliest of these staples was fish, followed by furs, timber, and dairy products. In 1870, agricultural products, fish, lumber, and timber accounted for nearly 85 percent of Canadian exports. In the first decade after 1900, wheat and other grains, woodpulp, and some metals (for example, nickel) also began to assume prominence in Canadian exports. Subsequently, the number and quantity of metals exported increased, and

[1]Among the best-known assessments of this kind over the past fifteen years are the series of publications by the Royal Commission on Canada's Economic Prospects, Ottawa, Queen's Printer, various years; W. T. Easterbrook and H. G. J. Aitken, *Canadian Economic History,* Toronto, Macmillan, 1958; Richard E. Caves and Richard H. Holton, *The Canadian Economy: Prospects and Retrospect,* Cambridge, Massachusetts, Harvard University Press, 1961; Gordon W. Bertram, "Historical Statistics on Growth and Structure of Manufacturing in Canada, 1870–1957," *Conferences on Statistics, 1962 & 1963: Papers,* ed. J. Henripin and A. Asimakopulos, Toronto, University of Toronto Press, 1964, pp. 93–146; and O. J. Firestone, *Canada's Economic Development 1867–1953,* London, Bowes and Bowes, 1958.

newsprint became significant. By 1926, wheat was the leading export, followed by newsprint, wheat flour, planks and boards, woodpulp, barley, and undressed fur skins, then by whiskey, farm implements, primary and semi-fabricated copper, pulpwood, and primary and semi-fabricated lead. With the exception of farm implements, all these top twelve exports either were resource products or relied on resources as their chief input. By 1952, fur skins, pulpwood, lead, and whiskey were no longer among the leading exports, having been replaced by four other staples—asbestos, primary and semi-fabricated aluminum, nickel, and zinc.[2]

Caves and Holton, in 1961,[3] described three important historical factors influencing the development of staples in Canadian production and export trade: (1) accidental discovery or purposeful exploration; (2) changing world market and demand conditions favouring Canadian sources of supply; and (3) technological developments enabling competitive exploitation of Canadian supplies. These forces have been operative in recent years too. We might note, as examples, the accidental discovery of immense potash reserves in Saskatchewan in the search for petroleum, as well as continuing oil finds in the Canadian West and North resulting from careful exploration programs. Or we could cite the rapid growth of U.S. and Japanese demands for energy, and technological advances permitting such developments as the utilization of the Athabasca tar sands and the economic extraction and shipment of Albertan coal to Japan.

The results have been that, in the last decade or so, two additional resource product groups—petroleum and natural gas and iron ore—have been among the main items shipped abroad. Potash and, most recent of all, coal have also risen in export significance.

The expansion of Canada's world trade in staples has in turn stimulated the growth of other sectors of the economy. A high correlation has been observed historically between Canada's exports in any one year and Canadian national income the following year.[4] The mechanism seems to have been that new exports have exerted a favourable effect on business investment and thus, through a multiplier-accelerator type of relationship, on national income. More particularly, the mounting production of staples has often involved strong backward linkages to other sectors of the economy serving the staple industries and forward linkages to sectors using the staples as inputs. Wheat, for example, required the construction of roads and railways and provided an incentive for the manufacture of agricultural implements

[2]DBS, *Canada Year Book, 1954*, Ottawa, Queen's Printer, 1954, p. 985; cited in Caves and Holton, *The Canadian Economy*, p. 386.
[3]Caves and Holton, *The Canadian Economy*, pp. 32–41.
[4]*Ibid.*, pp. 81–3.

and railway cars. One recent assessment of the wheat boom of 1901 to 1911, taking into account the wheat boom's dynamic stimulative effects on immigration, on economies of scale in manufacturing production, and on domestic saving, estimated that it was responsible for 28 percent of the total rise in per capita income for the period.[5] Other staples, such as minerals and petroleum and natural gas, while perhaps not having relatively as great an impact on the economy in recent years as the wheat boom had had just after the turn of the century, have nevertheless tended to display important linkages with other sectors, particularly those sectors using these staples in production.[6] The exploitation of petroleum and natural gas and hydro power has provided vital sources of energy for the growing economy.

The outcome has been that manufacturing has enjoyed a fairly steady growth since Confederation. Bertram's work placed the annual average compound rate of growth for 1870 to 1957 at 4.2 percent, with peaks in the 1900–10 period, in the decade following World War I, and in World War II.[7] Recent work by the Dominion Bureau of Statistics indicated that the compound annual growth rate of goods-producing industries for the period 1960–69 was 6.0 percent.[8] Lithwick estimated that between 1937 and 1961 the expansion of manufacturing "accounted for about one-third of the growth of aggregate output in Canada."[9]

This enlargement of the total manufacturing sector was accompanied by extensive diversification or filling out within the sector and by a growing absolute and relative importance of more sophisticated types of manufacture. Over the period studied by Bertram, 1870–1957, the growth rate for the primary or resource-based manufacturing industries was somewhat less than the average for all manufacturing (only 3.9 percent), while that for secondary manufacturing was a trifle higher than average (4.3 percent).[10] Table I offers crude evidence of the adjustments that were occurring. Increasing diversification is suggested by the progressively diminishing proportion that the top seven industries represented in the total of manufacturing during the course of the past century—diminishing from 85 percent in 1870 to 64 percent in 1967. The greater consequence of the more sophisticated industries is indicated by the appearance, in the top seven, of the chemical-products indus-

---

[5]Richard Caves, "Export-led Growth and the New Economic History," *Trade, Balance of Payments, and Growth: Papers in International Economics in Honor of Charles P. Kindleberger*, ed. J. Bhagwati *et al.*, Amsterdam, North Holland Publishing Co., 1971, pp. 403–42.
[6]Caves and Holton, *The Canadian Economy*, p. 44.
[7]Bertram, "Historical Statistics ...," Table 2, p. 103.
[8]*DBS Weekly*, February 19, 1971, Ottawa, Queen's Printer, p. 11.
[9]N. H. Lithwick, *Economic Growth in Canada: A Quantitative Analysis*, second edition, Toronto, University of Toronto Press, 1970, p. 33.
[10]Bertram, "Historical Statistics ...", Table 2, p. 103.

| % of mfg. value added | 1910 Name | % of mfg. value added | 1926 Name | % of mfg. value added | 1957 Name | % of mfg. value added | 1967[a] Name |
|---|---|---|---|---|---|---|---|
| 20.9 | Food and beverages | 17.1 | Food and beverages | 18.7 | Iron and steel products | 15.1 | Food and beverages |
| 16.8 | Wood products | 16.4 | Iron and steel products | 12.3 | Food and beverages | 14.6 | Transportation equipment |
| 16.3 | Iron and steel products | 14.0 | Paper products | 9.7 | Transportation equipment | 9.8 | Metal fabrication industries |
| 14.0 | Clothing | 8.6 | Wood products | 8.5 | Paper products | 8.7 | Paper products |
| 6.9 | Transportation equipment | 7.4 | Transportation equipment | 7.4 | Non-ferrous metal products | 6.2 | Primary metal |
| 6.8 | Non-ferrous metal products | 6.0 | Textiles (except clothing) | 6.4 | Chemical products | 6.2 | Chemical products |
| 3.7 | Leather products | 5.3 | Printing and publishing | 5.8 | Wood products | 6.0 | Electrical products |
| 85.4 | | 74.8 | | 68.8 | | 66.6 | |

ctly comparable with the earlier years because of changes in classification in 1960.
7: G. W. Bertram, "Historical Statistics on Growth and Structure of Manufacturing in Canada, 1870–1957," ssociation Conferences on Statistics 1962 and 1963: Papers, ed. J. Henripin and A. Asimakopulos, Toronto, Univ 4, pp. 112–13; 1967: DBS, 1967 Annual Census of Manufacturers: Preliminary Bulletin: Summary Statistics, Ottawa, –4.

tries in the 1957 and subsequent rankings and then of the electrical-products industries in the 1967 ranking. Although these industries had existed in earlier years, it was in the decade following World War I that they began to show noticeable gains in strength. The production of soaps, paints, and pharmaceuticals began in the 1920s, as did the production of washing machines, electric stoves, refrigerators, and radios. Also worth noting is the rise that occurred in rank of the transportation-equipment industries, now largely consisting of automobiles and parts and aircraft and parts.[11] Concomitantly, the labour-intensive clothing, other textiles, and leather-products industries have lost their places among the leading industries. The wood industries, which, like the foregoing three industries, involve fairly simple processing techniques, also have diminished in relative importance.

Food and beverages, on the one hand, and iron and steel products, on the other, have consistently been near the top over the years. The iron and steel category, up to 1960, contained a wide array of products—from iron castings and primary iron and steel to industrial machinery and agricultural implements. This category and that of non-ferrous-metals products (which had been the sixth largest industry in 1910 and the fifth largest manufacturing sector in 1957) were subdivided in the 1960 reclassification of industries into three groups—primary metals, metal-fabricating industries (excluding machinery industries), and machinery industries (excluding electrical machinery). The first two of these three groups both appear in the top-seven group for 1967.

The development of the pulp and paper (chiefly newsprint) industry has been aided by the abundance of hydro-electricity[12] in Canada and, more important, by the initiatives taken around the turn of the century by the provincial and federal governments in prohibiting and/or taxing the export of pulpwood to the United States. The eventual outcome of these policies was that the United States granted free entry for the lower grade of newsprint in their Underwood Tariff of 1913. By 1926 pulp and paper was the third largest manufacturing industry in Canada, and it was still fourth largest in 1967.

The history of this industry is instructive. Canada now takes for granted its role as a big pulp and paper exporter. But we should not forget that it was the strong stand on the need for processing in Canada taken by Canadians in international negotiations that was instrumental in enabling the country to move from being merely a large exporter of cut logs to U.S. paper mills to having a Canadian pulp and paper industry.[18]

[11]More will be said in the next section about the rapid augmentation of these industries.
[12]In 1966 the pulp and paper industry alone absorbed 16 percent of all electrical energy produced in the country. DBS, *Canada Year Book: 1968*, Ottawa, Queen's Printer, 1968, p. 662.
[18]The details of this industrial development, well-known to Canadian economists but

More will be said about the diversification of Canadian production and exports in a subsequent section. One further comment may, however, be made at this juncture.

Canadian growth and adaptation to changes in world market situations have meant that substantial structural shifts have been necessary within the domestic economy. As the industries of their employ declined, men and capital have had to move to new endeavours. Many of the adjustments have undoubtedly been painful for those concerned. Yet, while we recognize these personal costs, few people would want to turn back the clock to avoid the changes or obstruct the adaptations that occurred as the nation responded to domestic and international competitive forces – and prospered. Lithwick[14] showed that nearly 15 percent of the average annual growth of real output between 1937 and 1961 may be attributed to these shifts of labour and capital among industries. The most important of these interindustry shifts has been the movement out of agriculture in response to new farming technology and changes in world markets.

### The Canadian tariff

A characteristic that Canada has shared with most other developed and developing nations over the past hundred years or so has been the substantial protection afforded industry, especially secondary manufacturing. The history of Canadian protection has been reviewed briefly in Chapter 1.

In very recent years, if the level of tariffs is measured by the ratio of duty collected to total imports, the average is about 6½ percent—the lowest it has been at any time, at least in the last 125 years. When measured as the ratio of duty collected to dutiable imports, the present rate of barely over 16 percent is below that for every year back to before the Cayley-Galt tariffs of 1858–59 were imposed.

These recent averages, as well as rates according to major commodity classifications, are illustrated for 1968 in Table II. The high rates for the food, feed, beverages, and tobacco section are attributable to the importance of tobacco and alcoholic beverages. The latter commodity group accounted in 1968 for 46 percent of the tariffs collected on this section of products. Textile fabricated materials and chemicals together were responsible for 50 percent of the tariff revenue obtained from the fabricated-materials section and substantially raise the average duties for this group. For the sophisticated end products, duties collected were only 6 percent of total imports. This average

---

perhaps not to other readers, are summarized in H. G. J. Aitken, *The American Economic Impact on Canada*, Durham, North Carolina, Duke University Press, 1959.
[14]Lithwick, *Economic Growth in Canada*, Chap. 4, especially Table 26, p. 32.

TABLE II

DUTIES COLLECTED AS PERCENTAGE OF TOTAL IMPORTS
AND AS PERCENTAGE OF DUTIABLE IMPORTS, 1968[a]

| Commodity classification | As percentage of total imports | As percentage of dutiable imports |
|---|---|---|
| Live animals | 4.5 | 5.2 |
| Food, feed, beverages, and tobacco | 10.6 | 17.9 |
| Crude materials, inedible | 0.9 | 6.5 |
| Fabricated materials, inedible | 9.4 | 15.1 |
| End products, inedible | 6.0 | 17.4 |
| Special transactions—trade[b] | 13.0 | 15.3 |
| All products | 6.6 | 16.3 |

[a]Includes additional and special duties that cannot be allocated to any particular sections or commodities.
[b]Drawbacks have not been excluded. These normally amount to 0.3 or 0.4 percent of total import duties.
Source: DBS, *Trade of Canada*; and Canadian Tax Foundation, *The National Finances, 1969–70*, Toronto, 1969, Table 38, p. 58.

tends to be low primarily because of autos and parts entering the country tariff-free. Duties collected as a proportion of *dutiable* imports, however (17.4 percent in 1968), was more in line with expectations of what a nation's tariffs on highly manufactured goods, relative to crude and fabricated materials, would look like.

For the protective effect of tariffs on industry, duties on inputs into production processes must be considered in addition to duties on final products. That is, the *effective* protection—the percentage increase in *value added* made possible by the tariff structure—must be investigated. In tariff negotiations, even when average duties on imports are lowered, there may be little change in effective protection, simply because duties on both inputs and outputs are lowered simultaneously. The Canadian tariff cuts granted in the Kennedy Round tended to be of this type.[15] Effective rates in Canada remain in the neighbourhood of 30 percent for many manufacturing industries.[16]

*Canadian trade in the 1960s*

On the whole, Canadian trade in the past decade has flourished. From 1960–61 to 1968–69 exports and imports expanded at annual average compound rates of 11 percent and 10.1 percent, respectively. For the latter part

[15]J. R. Melvin and B. W. Wilkinson, *Effective Protection in the Canadian Economy*, Ottawa, Queen's Printer, 1968, pp. 23, 33–4. In a sample of thirty-two industries, effective protection was found actually to have increased in between 30 and 40 percent of the industries.
[16]*Ibid.*

of this period, 1964–65 to 1968–69, the growth rates were even faster—11.9 percent and 13.2 percent. In 1970, however, the effects of government measures to dampen the economy were much in evidence for imports. Imports declined slightly from the previous year, the first absolute decline since 1960. Export trade continued to prosper, however, rising by 13 percent over 1969.

The Canadian share of world exports recovered somewhat during the 1960s. By the end of the decade, Canada's export share hovered near 6 percent, a relative position not enjoyed since 1952–53. Canadian imports, at 5.6 percent of world trade, were once more at a relative level prevailing throughout much of the 1950s.

A. DEPENDENCE UPON THE UNITED STATES

A number of features of Canadian trade deserve emphasis in any discussion of future commercial-policy alternatives for the nation. The first of these is Canada's heavy dependence upon a single trading partner. At the end of the 1960s, 71 percent of all merchandise exports were destined for, and 73 percent of imports were from, the United States. For highly manfactured goods, the corresponding percentages were 87 and 81. Neither New Zealand's dependence upon the United Kingdom nor the dependence of any one country in the European Economic Community upon all the rest *taken as a group* is as great as Canada's dependence upon the United States.

This is not a new phenomenon. In the 1880s the United States supplanted Britain as Canada's main supplier,[17] and as early as 1929 nearly 69 percent of Canadian imports were from that country. On the export side, the United States began to replace Britain as Canada's chief market in the early 1920s, and since the middle of World War II the United States has been the undisputed leading purchaser of Canadian products.

Proximity to American sources of supply, exposure to American news and literature, economic scale and efficiency of U.S. production, American control of much of Canadian mining and manufacturing, and American technological leadership and aggressiveness have all contributed to the high proportion of Canadian imports coming from the United States. The abundance of Canadian raw materials, the huge demand for these resources by the U.S. industrial complex, the availability of American capital to exploit them (generally through ownership and control rather than debt capital), the desire to minimize transportation costs, and Canadian political stability have made Canada a logical source of crude materials for the United States. These

[17]This information and subsequent historical facts are from M. C. Urquhart and K. Buckley, *Historical Statistics of Canada,* Toronto, The Macmillan Company of Canada, 1965, p. 182.

considerations, combined with the traditional Canadian myopia when it comes to seeking foreign markets for all products, including highly manufactured goods, make the heavy concentration of the nation's exports to the United States not at all surprising.

Historically, only the tariff preferences that Canada exchanged with British Commonwealth countries (commencing in 1896 with the United Kingdom) have operated in the opposite direction to the previously mentioned forces. But with Britain suffering the shock of two world wars, overvaluation of the pound in the 1920s, and a lack of promotional effort and adaptability in meeting changing consumer demands, the effect of these preferences has not been sufficient to outweigh the many other determinants of trade working in favour of the United States. The preferences have been eroded too by the successive rounds of GATT tariff reductions, as well as by the effects of inflation on specific (as opposed to *ad valorem*) rates of duty.

During the 1960s the most important determinant of the increase in trade dependence on the United States was federal government policies designed primarily to improve the efficiency and to hasten the diversification of Canadian manufacturing. One important measure was the Canada-United States Defence Production Sharing Program, commenced in 1959. About 38 percent of all non-edible finished-product exports (excluding automobiles and parts) exported to the United States since 1959 came under this agreement. Most of the products were aerospace and communications equipment.

A more dramatic example of government policy's effect in expanding Canadian trade ties with the United States is the well-known Canada-U.S. auto pact of January, 1965, providing for tariff-free shipments of autos and parts (other than replacement parts) between manufacturers[18] in the two countries. The product flows emanating from this agreement have dominated Canada's trade picture for the last half of the 1960s. From 1965 to 1970 imports from the United States of automobiles and parts rose from 7 percent to 22 percent of all Canadian imports. Exports of these products to that country grew from .2 percent to 20 percent of total exports. Moreover, the deficit of $781 million on auto trade with the United States in 1965 became a surplus of $196 million in 1971. The rationalization of industry resulting from the pact has made it possible for Canada to export more automobiles, trucks, and parts to other countries, such as Latin America, as well, although these increments are small, in both relative and absolute terms, compared to the expansion of bilateral Canada-U.S. flows.

Also working in the direction of Canadian reliance on the United States

[18]Private citizens do not enjoy this privilege. Hence the agreement cannot be considered one of sectoral free trade. There are also certain stipulations to be met by the companies as to Canadian content in production.

(although the quantitative impact has undoubtedly been much less for Canada than that of the auto agreement) has been the tendency towards insulation of the North American market from Pacific (including Latin American) sources of labour-intensive products. Witness the quantitative restrictions placed upon textile and clothing exports to Canada and the United States as a direct consequence of representations by the Canadian and U.S. governments. These "voluntary" export restraints have undoubtedly slowed down the rate of increase in Canadian imports of such goods from these countries—and probably of other labour-intensive commodities as well—and they may also have made it easier for Canadian suppliers of fashion goods to enter the American market, as they have in recent years.

Apart from these measures, there is reason to believe that in the past ten to fifteen years the strength of certain of the historical forces favouring imports from the United States has been declining. The formation of the European Economic Community and the European Free Trade Association has increased the efficiency and competitiveness of European producers. While the United States is still the technological leader in many fields, the European industrialized countries and Japan have recognized that, by concentrating their industrial research and development efforts in limited areas and by specializing in production, they can compete successfully in foreign markets. Their lower wage rates are an additional factor in their favour, provided the competitive advantage of these lower rates is not more than offset by lower productivity. The coming revolution in air transport costs will further reduce the significance of the proximity of the United States as a deciding factor in gaining Canadian markets.

These considerations, combined with the systematic way in which the Japanese and, to a lesser extent, some European nations are expanding their shares of the Canadian market, suggest that in the absence of further special arrangements (or even a full free trade agreement) between Canada and the United States, some decline in the American share of Canadian imports may take place. Some support for this position is offered in Table III. Imports from Japan, the EEC, and EFTA nations other than Britain grew faster between 1960 and 1970 than did imports from the United States. And if it had not been for the auto pact, Canadian imports from every nation or trading group shown in the table, with the exception of Britain, would have increased faster than imports from the United States.

The future distribution of Canadian exports is less clear. On the one hand, the rapidly growing demand for crude and semi-fabricated materials by the developed European nations and Japan suggests that these markets will become of increasing relative significance to Canada. Table III shows that shipments to Japan have shown the greatest percentage increase of exports

TABLE III

COUNTRY DISTRIBUTION OF CANADIAN EXPORTS AND IMPORTS, 1960, 1969, 1970, AND 1970 TRADE AS A PERCENTAGE OF 1960

| | Percentage distribution | | | |
| --- | --- | --- | --- | --- |
| | 1960 | 1969 | 1970 | 1970/1960 |
| *Exports* | | | | |
| EFTA | 19.3 | 9.0 | 10.7 | 1.7 |
| Excluding the United Kingdom | 2.3 | 1.5 | 1.8 | 2.5 |
| United Kingdom | 17.0 | 7.6 | 8.9 | 1.6 |
| EEC | 8.1 | 5.8 | 7.1 | 2.7 |
| Japan | 3.3 | 4.3 | 4.7 | 4.5 |
| United States | 54.4 | 70.7 | 65.1 | 3.8 |
| Excluding autos | 54.2 | 50.0 | 45.2 | 2.6 |
| Autos | 0.2 | 20.7 | 19.9 | 279.4 |
| All other countries | 14.8 | 10.1 | 12.4 | 2.6 |
| Total | 100.0 | 100.0 | 100.0 | 3.1 |
| *Imports* | | | | |
| EFTA | 12.0 | 7.7 | 7.6 | 1.6 |
| Excluding the United Kingdom | 1.3 | 2.1 | 2.3 | 4.7 |
| United Kingdom | 10.7 | 5.6 | 5.3 | 1.3 |
| EEC | 5.3 | 5.1 | 5.8 | 2.8 |
| Japan | 2.0 | 3.5 | 4.2 | 5.3 |
| United States | 67.2 | 72.6 | 71.1 | 2.7 |
| Excluding autos | 60.1 | 51.8 | 49.3 | 2.1 |
| Autos | 7.1 | 20.8 | 21.7 | 7.7 |
| All other countries | 13.4 | 11.1 | 11.3 | 2.2 |
| Total | 100.0 | 100.0 | 100.0 | 2.5 |

Source: DBS, *Trade of Canada*, various years.

to any country over the past decade. And if automotive trade with America is set aside, exports to the EEC also have risen more rapidly than shipments to America. But Americans' demands for materials are also growing fast, and their manoeuvering to gain access to Canadian energy and water supplies on the same terms on which these supplies are made available to Canadian users (i.e., some form of Canada-U.S. energy pact) may mean that Canada will continue to ship a growing proportion of its total exports to the United States. At the time of writing, it is too early to say what the net outcome of these various influences will be.

B. THE COMMODITY COMPOSITION OF TRADE

A second relevant characteristic of Canadian trade when we think of future commercial-policy alternatives for Canada is its commodity composition. On the one hand, imports are largely of a highly manufactured nature. On the other hand, although sophisticated products have been the most dynamic sector in exports over the 1960s, raw and semi-processed shipments still pre-

TABLE IV

CANADA'S IMPORTS AND EXPORTS BY STAGE OF FABRICATION, 1960 AND 1970
(percentages based on current dollars)

| | Exports | | | Imports | | |
|---|---|---|---|---|---|---|
| | Percentage distribution | | | Percentage distribution | | |
| | 1960 (1) | 1970 (2) | 1970/1960 (3) | 1960 (4) | 1970 (5) | 1970/1960 (6) |
| Foodstuffs, crude materials and semi-processed goods | 88.4 | 62.8 | 2.3 | 42.8 | 32.1 | 1.9 |
| Animals, food, feed, beverage, and tobacco | *18.8* | *11.3* | *1.9* | *10.6* | *8.0* | *1.9* |
| Crude materials, inedible | *21.2* | *18.2* | *2.8* | *13.6* | *8.4* | *1.6* |
| Fabricated materials, inedible*a* | *48.4* | *33.3* | *2.2* | *18.6* | *15.7* | *2.1* |
| Highly manufactured goods*b* | 11.3 | 37.0 | 10.5 | 55.4 | 66.7 | 3.1 |
| Excluding road motor vehicles | *10.1* | *15.6* | *4.3* | *45.1* | *43.5* | *2.4* |
| Road motor vehicles | *1.2* | *21.4* | *57.4* | *10.3* | *23.2* | *5.7* |
| Special transactions*c* | 0.3 | 0.2 | 2.5 | 1.9 | 1.2 | 1.6 |
| Total*d* | 100.0 | 100.0 | 3.2 | 100.0 | 100.0 | 2.5 |

*a*Fabricated materials, inedible, from *Trade of Canada*, less chemicals and chemical products.
*b*End products, inedible, from *Trade of Canada*, plus chemicals and chemical products.
   *c*Items less than $200 and other goods not classified.
   *d*Totals may not add due to rounding.
Source: DBS, *Trade of Canada*, 1960 and 1970 issues.

dominate (Table IV). Imports and exports will be considered in turn, but the emphasis will be placed upon highly manufactured exports for two reasons. The Canadian potential for them does not appear to be realized as fully as for primary-product shipments, and it is this sector that will be most affected by changes in domestic and foreign trade restrictions.

*Imports.* Highly manufactured commodities account for two-thirds of total imports. (In contrast, the remaining OECD countries as a group have only about 37 percent of their total imports in the highly manufactured category.)[19] Within this broad group, imports of automobiles and parts, making up 23 percent of total imports, have been expanding the fastest during the 1960s. The next most rapidly growing divisions have been jet aircraft and machinery—products based on advanced technology.

[19]The definition used covers all end products, inedible, in *Trade of Canada*, plus chemicals and chemical products. The relevant SITC groups are 7, 8, 54, 55, and 57.

Of the raw and semi-processed group, fuels and lubricants, although only 6 percent of total imports, registered the most rapid increase of any commodity division over the 1960s. Between the mid-1950s and the early 1960s, this was one of the slowest growing categories of imports because the markets of western Canada and the major part of Ontario were being taken over by Canadian crude in accordance with the provisions of the national oil policy. Once this supply realignment had been accomplished, however, the remaining markets—that is, everything east of the Ottawa River (including Montreal), accounting for over one-half of Canadian requirements—were still in a position to satisfy their needs from imported crude, primarily from Venezuela.[20]

*Highly manufactured exports.* In 1970, even after the tremendous upsurge in automotive shipments abroad and even though exports of other sophisticated manufactures grew faster than exports of raw or fabricated materials during the 1960s, highly manufactured goods still comprised only 37 percent of exports (Table IV). Sixty percent of highly manufactured exports (or nearly 22 percent of all exports) were automotive products. (The remainder included a wide range of machinery, including farm machinery, communication and navigation equipment, and aircraft.) Hence, not only did well below 50 percent of exports consist of sophisticated manufactures, but this category also relied heavily on a single product group. (The other OECD countries taken together had 50 percent of their exports in similar products and only 9 percent of their total exports concentrated in automobiles and parts.)

The main explanation for the relatively small participation of Canadian secondary manufacturing in international trade has been expressed in terms of tariffs and economies of scale. The hypothesis, in brief, is that the Canadian tariff has provided a sheltered market within which domestic and foreign-owned firms have established themselves. The "bandwagon" effect has resulted in more foreign firms entering in any one industry than are really required to serve the domestic market. Hence their plants and domestic-owned plants either have been too small to be efficient or have been producing too many lines to achieve the lowest possible costs. Foreign tariffs are seen as important barriers to export. Rationalization of industry has tended not to occur spontaneously, because domestic-owned firms have been unwilling to take on international giants in price wars or other marketing wars that they might not win. Foreign-owned firms have hesitated to activate hostilities that might spread to their parents and affiliates abroad. Content-

---

[20]This substantial growth of imports has occurred even though the potential flow from Albertan wells is more than sufficient to satisfy eastern demands. The world price of imported crude was less than the price that the international oil companies have decreed for western Canadian crude piped to the Montreal market.

ment with serving the domestic market and limited interest in world markets have become the order of the day.

In the last decade, attempts to explain the strong showing of secondary manufactured exports have centred on the removal of domestic and foreign (American) tariffs and on the attainment of scale economies in certain sectors. The defence production sharing agreement and the auto pact are the striking examples generally cited. Because of these arrangements (and the earlier removal of tariffs on agricultural machinery),[21] between 75 and 80 percent of Canadian exports of sophisticated manufactures to America enter that country tariff-free.[22] Since shipments to the United States account for between 85 and 90 percent of total Canadian exports of such products, this means that about two-thirds of all of Canada's highly manufactured exports to the world go to the United States without the hindrance of tariffs and therefore presumably make it easier for Canadian producers to achieve scale economies.

But the argument in terms of tariffs and economies of scale is not the sole explanation of export achievement (or a lack thereof, as the case may be). Nor, on occasion, is it necessarily the most important one. The fact of faster growth during the sixties of highly manufactured exports than of other exports extends beyond those commodities enjoying tariff-free access to foreign markets and includes a wide range of electrical products, machinery, and industrial equipment. Improved credit and insurance facilities that the federal government has provided for exporters have undoubtedly been important in helping exporters to offer terms competitive with those offered by foreign firms. But even after the statistics on highly manufactured exports are adjusted for the possible influence of such export credits—as well as for the defence production sharing arrangement, the auto pact, and the rapid expansion of the American economy throughout the 1960s—there is still a "residual" increase in exports that is "unexplained." Other influences have apparently been at work.[23]

The most obvious other factor is the depreciation of the Canadian dollar to U.S.92.5 cents that occurred during 1961–62 and prevailed until June, 1970, when a flexible exchange rate was adopted. But a number of associated influences too may have played a role. Canadian manufacturing industries,

[21]The American tariffs were eliminated in 1913 with the exception of the tariff on tractors for certain uses. But the rationalization in Canada did not really commence until Canadian tariff removal in 1944 provided the necessary spur to change.
[22]About 67 percent is road motor vehicles and parts, 7–9 percent consists of aerospace and communications equipment, and 3–4 percent is farm machinery.
[23]B. W. Wilkinson, *Canada's International Trade: An Analysis of Recent Trends and Patterns,* Montreal, Canadian Trade Committee, 1968, Chap. 4. Updating of this work for the latter one-half of the 1960s did not alter the conclusion.

as a consequence of the filling-out process that had been continuing over the decades, simply may have reached a stage of maturity enabling them to compete successfully abroad. More important, the excess capacity that prevailed in the late 1950s, when the Canadian dollar was at a premium and there was consequently pressure on manufacturers to improve their efficiency and cut costs, probably helped to prepare them to take advantage of the strengthened competitive position offered by a lower Canadian exchange value.

Trade-promotion fairs abroad, "export" conferences at home, and greater informational services to actual and potential exporters by provincial and federal governments may have helped alert firms to the opportunities already existing for sales in other lands.

The last two explanations—the cost-cutting that manufacturers were forced into while the Canadian dollar was overvalued in the late 1950s and the awakening of manufacturers to the possibilities for sales abroad by the publicity and promotional activities of governments—amount to a distinct implication that there had been major inefficiencies in Canadian production that could have been eliminated earlier had management taken the necessary initiatives. If we argue that there may have been a demonstration effect from the defence production sharing or auto agreements which dramatized the advantages, for firms operating in Canada, of rationalizing production and making exports a normal part of their operations, we are again saying the same thing. This is also true if we hypothesize that the manufacturing community may have begun to take seriously, and act upon, the message of economists over the past fifteen years that there are inefficiencies in Canadian production attributable to inadequate specialization[24] and that, because wages in Canada have generally been, and in some sectors still are, considerably lower than in the United States, a substantial increase in Canadian productivity would permit competitive trade with the United States in spite of the remaining American tariffs.[25]

More generally, such views can be summarized in the proposition that management initiative and enterprise, be it in foreign- or domestically-owned firms, is a key determinant of the export performance of industry.

The deficiencies of management have been identified by Caves as having been a crucial element in the stagnation of the British economy.[26] Leiben-

---

[24]See Sperry Lea, "Some Economic Aspects of Canadian-U.S. Relations," Conference on Canadian-U.S. Relations, Wingspread, 1969, p. I-9.
[25]Provided that international unions do not immediately force up Canadian wages.
[26]Richard Caves and associate, "Market Organization, Performance and Public Policy," *Britain's Economic Prospects*, Washington, Brookings Institution, 1968, pp. 279–323, especially pp. 300–6.

stein[27] has provided empirical testimony for a number of countries of firms' "X-inefficiency" or the extent to which they are not getting the maximum possible output from their inputs. More recently he has proffered a type of behavioural theory of why so much X-inefficiency exists.[28]

The quality of management permeates every aspect of a firm's attainment. It will influence not only whether realizable economies of scale in production are achieved and new markets explored, but also whether research and development is undertaken with the object of developing distinctive, high-quality, competitive products. As noted earlier, new technology and the product differentiation that results have now been recognized as prime determinants of international trade in sophisticated products.[29] Although Canadian industrial research is miniscule compared with that of the United States and a number of other developed nations, the evidence intimates that Canadian secondary manufacturing exports, as a proportion of domestic production, tend to be significantly larger in those industries where research and development have been relatively more important.[30] Moreover, Safarian[31] has noted that foreign subsidiaries that export a large proportion of their sales are more likely to have products differentiated from those of their parent companies abroad, and tend to undertake relatively more research and development in Canada, than firms exporting less.

Another factor of significance in export performance is economies of scale in marketing. It is no coincidence that the strongest export accomplishments in Canadian manufacturing—for example, in machinery and electrical equipment[32]—have occurred in investment-goods industries, where certain marketing peculiarities obtain: the number of purchasers that must be reached in any country is relatively small, and sales are often made directly to the manufacturer, so that there is avoidance of the commissions of middlemen, the need for large selling organizations, and expensive advertising. That is, gains have been greatest in industries where it has not been necessary to achieve massive sales before unit marketing costs could be reduced to competitive levels.

[27]"Allocative Efficiency vs. 'X-Efficiency'," American Economic Review, June 1966, pp. 392–432.
[28]H. Leibenstein, "Organizational or Frictional Equilibria, X-Efficiency, and the Rate of Innovation," Quarterly Journal of Economics, Nov. 1969, pp. 600–23.
[29]See Raymond Vernon, ed., The Technology Factor in International Trade, New York, National Bureau of Economic Research, 1970.
[30]Wilkinson, Canada's International Trade, Chap. 7; see also D. A. Drinkwalter, "Some Economic Characteristics of Canadian Exporting Firms," Ph.D. dissertation, University of Western Ontario, 1971.
[31]A. E. Safarian, The Performance of Foreign-Owned Firms in Canada, Montreal and Washington, Canadian-American Committee, 1969, Chaps. 4 and 5.
[32]Wilkinson, Canada's International Trade, Chap. 7.

*Other exports.* Crude materials and semi-processed commodities comprise about 30 percent and 33 percent, respectively, of Canadian exports. That is, nearly two-thirds of exports still reflect a comparative advantage in natural-resource-based products. Several features of this trade warrant comment. First, crude-material exports have been rising more rapidly than have exports of fabricated materials, with the pace being set by crude petroleum and natural gas, iron ore, nickel, copper and other ores, and, more recently, coal. Second, Canada has been exporting both the raw materials and the energy resources needed to process them—petroleum and natural gas to the United States and coal to Japan. Low foreign tariffs on these material and fuel inputs, coupled with high tariffs on finished products, have strongly encouraged this pattern. Third, grains, especially wheat, long a mainstay of Canadian sales abroad, showed relatively weak expansion during the sixties. This was undoubtedly partly because such trade had been neglected by federal authorities. Not until an agricultural crisis existed, with a stockpile of close to one billion bushels and grain exports down to their lowest value since 1960, were new government initiatives taken to extend liberal credit policies to foreign buyers and to aggressively seek out new buyers. Also, of course, the extreme agricultural protectionism of Japan, the European Economic Community, and, to a lesser extent, the United States has discouraged Canadian shipments to these markets and to third countries supplied by subsidized products from farmers in these nations.

## C. FOREIGN OWNERSHIP

Another relevant characteristic of the economy and of the nation's international trade is the significant foreign ownership ties. As of 1968, 74 percent of all mining and 65 percent of manufacturing in Canada were under foreign *control*.[33] (American firms accounted for about 70 percent of the total.) In other sectors the degree of foreign control is not as great, but has tended to rise. Of total assets *for all industries in the economy,* foreigners controlled 28.7 percent in 1965 and 31.1 percent in 1968.

Data on the proportions of Canadian trade accounted for by foreign-owned and -controlled companies are incomplete, but the numbers available clearly indicate that the proportions are large. For 1967, non-financial firms with assets of more than $5 million and with at least half their voting shares owned by foreign parent companies were responsible for 41 percent of Cana-

---

[33]DBS, *Corporations and Labour Unions Returns Act, Part 1,* 1968, Ottawa, Queen's Printer, 1970. These percentages are based on the assumption that 25 percent ownership of voting stock is sufficient for control. Even if 50 percent ownership is deemed necessary for control, foreign firms would still be in charge of 63 percent of all mining and 58 percent of all manufacturing.

dian exports and 38 percent of imports.[34] These large foreign-owned firms accounted for only 70 percent of the sales of all foreign-owned firms in mining and manufacturing companies and 60 percent of the sales of all foreign-owned non-financial companies.[35] If it is assumed that the smaller foreign-owned firms, which are not required to report, exported the same proportion of their total sales, and imported the same proportion of their total purchases, as did the reporting firms, then it can be calculated that nearly 66 percent of Canada's total exports and 58 percent of total imports were accounted for by foreign subsidiaries.[36] The proportions would be less than these numbers suggest if the smaller companies engaged less in foreign trade than the bigger ones—which seems likely. But then again, since foreign *control* is often exercised with under 50 percent of the voting stock, the proportions of total trade by foreign-*controlled* firms would be even greater than the numbers suggest. To the extent that these two considerations offset one another, the percentages provide a reasonable approximation to foreign participation in Canada's international commerce.

The reporting companies also indicated that 67 percent of their exports and 70 percent of their imports were with parents or affiliates abroad.[37] Applying these percentages to the preceding ones, we can *estimate that 44 percent of Canada's total exports and 40 percent of total imports* were accounted for by the shipment of products between parents and subsidiaries. If we were able to allow for the additional trade by *Canadian*-owned multinational corporations with their subsidiaries and affiliates abroad, we could see that the proportion of Canadian trade not passing through the market place by arm's-length bargaining, but simply being intra-corporate transfers of products, would certainly be in the neighbourhood of one-half the total of Canada's trade. In assessing in subsequent chapters the results of the empirical and theoretical analysis of the possible impact of alternate free trade arrangements, these corporate ties must be kept firmly in mind.

### Concluding observations[38]

The foregoing features of Canadian trade in the sixties (as well as the knowledge that the labour-force growth rate over the next half-dozen years or

[34]Government of Canada, Department of Industry, Trade and Commerce, *Foreign-Owned Subsidiaries in Canada, 1964–1967*, Ottawa, Queen's Printer, 1970, pp. 5, 10, and 12.
[35]*Ibid.*, p. 5.
[36]Derived using *ibid.*, p. 5, and *ibid.*, Summary Tables 1, 2, 4, and 5, pp. 10–13.
[37]*Ibid.*, p. 24.
[38]Material in this section was published earlier in B. W. Wilkinson, "Economic Cooperation in the Pacific: A Canadian Approach," *Journal of Common Market Studies*, 9, June 1971, 309.

so will be one of the highest of any developed country and will therefore require the rapid creation of many new jobs) suggest that those planning the nation's international economic policies for the seventies might well keep in mind the following objectives:

(1) reduction of foreign protectionism on agricultural commodities;

(2) greater utilization of Canadian energy and other natural resources in processing prior to export;

(3) continued and, if possible, accelerated rationalization and modernization of Canadian manufacturing to meet international competition at home and abroad; this should be accompanied by attention to new product and process development, aggressive marketing, and the implications of a sizable proportion of trade being intra-corporate transfers; and

(4) diversification of export markets and supply sources, so as to lower the present enormous reliance upon the United States.

# 3. The Growth of World Markets and Changing Trade Patterns

The close of the Second World War marked the beginning of a new era in international trade. The downward trend in world trade relative to world output that had characterized the prior three decades of the twentieth century was reversed, and trade began to expand more rapidly than the growth of output. Initial expectations were that this reversal was a temporary phenomenon which would disappear once postwar reconstruction was largely completed and traditional economic forces were permitted to reassert themselves. But gradually, as world trade and output records were compiled year after year, such expectations faded, to be replaced, first, by a hesitant optimism that the future held promise of a continued expansion of world trade more rapid than the surge of new output and, subsequently, by a conviction that, given appropriate liberalizing policies by the major nations of the world, this trend could characterize world markets for years to come. Since the outset of the 1970s, some clouds have gathered on the horizon, and the voice of concern about the future course of world trade is once more being heard. Yet there are powerful economic forces that may help to disperse the clouds and the concerned voices.

The foregoing remarks portend what this chapter is about. Its objective is to examine briefly Canada's past and present trading environments and from this examination to acquire a glimpse (admittedly an imperfect glimpse) of the world trade and commercial situation to which Canada will have to accommodate itself in the future.[1]

*Trends in world trade*

The broad trends in world trade and output over the past one hundred years are well known. Yet there is value in summarizing these trends quantitatively so that the present performance of the world economy will be brought

[1]This chapter is based upon D. W. Slater, *World Trade and Economic Growth: Trends and Prospects with Application to Canada*, PPAC series "Canada in the Atlantic Economy," no. 1, Toronto, University of Toronto Press, 1968, with additions from other sources as indicated in tables and footnotes.

TABLE I

WORLD TRENDS IN POPULATION, PRODUCTION, AND TRADE, 1876–1969:
SELECTED GROWTH RATES (compound annual rates in percentages)

| | | Production | | Trade volume | |
|---|---|---|---|---|---|
| Period | Population | Manufactures | Primary produce | Manufactures | Primary produce |
| 1876–80 to 1911–13 | 0.7 | 4.0 | n.a. | 4.0 | 4.0 |
| 1911–13 to 1926–30 | 0.7 | 2.5 | 1.7 | 1.2 | 1.5 |
| 1926–30 to 1934–35 | 1.3 | −1.0 | 0.3 | −5.1 | −1.4 |
| 1934–35 to 1948–50 | 1.3 | 4.0 | 1.5 | 3.1 | 0.1 |
| 1948–50 to 1957–59 | 1.5 | 5.4 | 3.0 | 7.4 | 5.4 |
| 1957–59 to 1963–65 | 1.8 | 6.0 | 2.4 | 8.2 | 5.4 |
| 1963–65 to 1967–69 | 2.1 | 6.8 | 3.0 | 9.9 | 5.0 |

Source: First six rows from D. W. Slater, *World Trade and Economic Growth: Trends and Prospects with Applications to Canada*, PPAC series "Canada in the Atlantic Economy," no. 1, Toronto, University of Toronto Press, 1968, Tables I and II. Seventh row calculated from GATT, *International Trade, 1969*, Geneva, 1970, and United Nations, *Monthly Bulletin of Statistics*.

into sharp relief. Table I is presented for this purpose. The fairly strong and similar growth rates of total production and trade up to the First World War; the slower rate of growth in the early 1920s, leading to a collapse and absolute decline in the first half of the 1930s; the revival thereafter; and the surge forward throughout the 1950s and 1960s are all portrayed.

Both manufactures and primary products followed these broad trends, although, as the table suggests, the comparative performance of the two groups in real terms has differed on occasion. Particularly noteworthy is that the volume of both output and trade declined more rapidly for manufactures than for primary products during the period from the late 1920s to the mid-1930s and that manufactures revived more rapidly than primary products thereafter.

Price trends were in contrast to the volume trends. The early 1930s witnessed a much more dramatic drop-off in prices of primary products than in prices of manufactures, while the immediate postwar years saw a much bigger revival in prices for primary products than for manufactures. Consequently, by the end of the 1940s primary products constituted about the same proportion of the value of world trade as they had done in the years from 1876 to the late 1920s. In the past two decades, however, trends in prices have followed those in volumes, so that the value of manufactures trade has moved steadily ahead of the value of primary-products trade. Hence the possibility seems remote for a return to some historically stable relationship between the value shares of trade in primary and manufactured commodities.

Within each of these two broad categories, considerable variation has occurred in the trade performance of individual product groups. Among primary commodities, petroleum trade has led the way for some decades, being the only major commodity registering substantial increases in volume and value between the late 1920s and the 1950s. But even its growth—in either volume or value terms—has not matched that of manufactures in the period since the Second World War. Trade in ores and concentrates has also expanded more rapidly than has trade for all primary manufactures. At the other end of the scale are agricultural raw materials and cereals. Livestock products have historically been a poor performer as well, although there have been spasmodic signs of improvement in recent years.

On the manufacturing side, between the late 1920s and the 1950s machinery, transportation equipment, and chemicals, in that order, were the fastest-growing sectors in volume terms. In value terms, the growth rate of the latter two groups was somewhat lower because of smaller price increases for them than for total manufacturing. Over the same period, metals and other manufactured commodities (such as newsprint, plywood, watches, and technical instruments) showed increases in volume approximating the average for all manufactures, while metal products other than those included in machinery and equipment expanded not at all. Trade in textiles and clothing actually declined slightly in volume.

During the 1960s trade growth in transportation equipment topped the list in value and volume terms, with the pace being set by automotive trade between Canada and the United States as a consequence of the rationalization stemming from the Canada-U.S. auto pact. Chemicals were close behind, followed by machinery and equipment. Iron and steel and miscellaneous manufactures again grew in volume terms roughly in step with the average for total manufacturing, while non-ferrous metals and textiles and clothing trade remained the slowest-growing sectors. The changing importance of these various product groups over the 1960s is indicated in Table II.

Given the more rapid growth of production and trade in manufactured products, particularly those reflecting advanced technology, than in primary products over the past two decades, and the concentration of manufacturing in the developed nations, it is not surprising that these nations should have expanded their value share of world exports from 59 percent in 1953 to 69 percent in 1969. Moreover, with these countries also possessing the bulk of the spending power, it is natural that trade among them would be increasing more quickly than either trade between them and the developing nations or trade among the developing nations themselves. To illustrate, between 1953 and 1969 exports from the industrially advanced nations to one another rose from 37 percent to 51 percent of the total value of world

TABLE II

WORLD EXPORTS, 1963, 1966, AND 1969, BY MAJOR
COMMODITY GROUP, AS PERCENTAGES OF TOTAL EXPORT
VALUES[a] (based on current dollar values)

| | Percentage of total exports | | |
|---|---|---|---|
| | 1963 | 1966 | 1969 |
| Primary products | 42.2 | 38.2 | 33.7 |
| Food | 19.5 | 17.8 | 14.8 |
| Raw materials | 9.3 | 7.8 | 6.6 |
| Ores and minerals | 3.2 | 3.2 | 3.2 |
| Fuels | 10.2 | 9.3 | 9.1 |
| Manufactures | 55.9 | 60.0 | 64.4 |
| Non-ferrous metals | 3.1 | 4.0 | 4.0 |
| Iron and steel | 4.8 | 4.8 | 5.0 |
| Chemicals | 6.1 | 6.7 | 7.1 |
| Engineering products | 20.4 | 21.7 | 22.9 |
| Road motor vehicles | 4.7 | 5.5 | 7.1 |
| Textiles and clothing | 6.0 | 5.9 | 6.0 |
| Other manufactures | 10.8 | 11.4 | 12.3 |
| Residue | 1.8 | 1.8 | 1.9 |
| Total exports | 100.0 | 100.0 | 100.0 |

[a]Totals may not add owing to rounding.
Source: 1969: GATT, *International Trade, 1969*, Table 7,
p. 21; 1965: GATT, *International Trade, 1968*, Geneva,
1969, Table 31, p. 115.

trade. In contrast, over the same period exports from developing nations
to the advanced countries dropped from 19 percent to 13 percent of world
trade, and exports from developing nations to one another decreased from
7 percent to 4 percent of world commerce.[2]

The most rapid trade growth of any developed country has been registered by Japan.[3] From 1955 to 1969 the value of exports expanded at an
annual rate of nearly 16 percent, increasing Japan's share of world exports
from 2 to 6.6 percent. Imports grew at nearly 14 percent annually, thereby
swelling the Japanese share of world imports from 2.3 percent to 5.6
percent. (These rates of expansion of trade were even greater than the rise
in Japanese GNP over the same period, which amounted to over 10 percent
annually.) Contrary to the situation for most of the developed countries,
Japan's rapid trade expansion has been with developing as well as developed
nations. In 1969, only about 50 percent of its total trade (exports and

[2]GATT, *International Trade*, various years. The remainder of world trade is by the
Eastern trading countries or Communist bloc.
[3]See GATT reports and Japan, Ministry of Foreign Affairs, *Statistical Survey of Japan's
Economy*, 1970.

TABLE III

TRADE OF MAJOR INDUSTRIAL AREAS, 1969 AS PERCENTAGE OF 1963 (based on current dollars)

| | Exports to | | | | Imports from | | | |
|---|---|---|---|---|---|---|---|---|
| | World excluding region | World | Indus-trial countries | The region itself | World excluding region | World | Indus-trial countries | The region itself |
| *Primary* *Products* | | | | | | | | |
| North America | 119.7 | 126.8 | 134.8 | 148.5 | 127.6 | 134.8 | 154.7 | 156.3 |
| EEC | 134.8 | 171.9 | 180.4 | 206.8 | 141.0 | 155.7 | 164.9 | 210.6 |
| EFTA | 128.9 | 131.5 | 132.4 | 137.4 | 114.8 | 117.8 | 122.1 | 137.3 |
| Japan | — | 180.3 | 115.6 | — | — | 208.8 | 186.9 | — |
| *Manufactures* | | | | | | | | |
| North America | 169.5 | 205.4 | 233.5 | 293.0 | 256.8 | 274.7 | 276.9 | 300.5 |
| EEC | 191.7 | 210.0 | 217.5 | 237.6 | 197.9 | 223.6 | 220.5 | 243.4 |
| EFTA | 161.5 | 172.7 | 190.6 | 216.5 | 186.2 | 195.3 | 195.8 | 220.9 |
| Japan | — | 305.5 | 352.9 | — | — | 265.8 | 224.6 | — |

Source: GATT, *International Trade, 1969*, Appendix Tables A, B, C, D.

imports) was with the nations of Western Europe, North America, and Oceania. But in line with the trade of developed countries, Japan has shifted away from dependence upon labour-intensive commodities such as textiles and clothing and has increased its emphasis upon capital-intensive products such as ships, sophisticated consumer durables, chemicals, iron and steel, and industrial machinery.

Apart from Japanese trade, the fastest growth in the trade of developed nations has been among the nations of Western Europe (particularly within the EEC[4] and, to a lesser extent, within EFTA) and between Canada and the United States. Numbers evidencing these changes for recent years are shown in Table III. This table also illustrates how the highly protectionist Common Agricultural Policy of the EEC (instituted in July, 1962) has made for much faster growth of primary-products trade within the EEC than between it and other nations.

Among the developing countries, those selling ores and concentrates, tropical foodstuffs, and, most important of all, crude petroleum did relatively better than those relying on non-tropical foodstuffs and non-mineral raw materials. Also, those enjoying some preferential treatment from particular developed nations (e.g., Britain or EEC countries) seemed to do better than other primary producers.

[4]Italy, with the best trade performance of the EEC countries, experienced increases in its foreign trade close to those of Japan—about 14 percent annually from 1955 to 1969.

*Trade-expanding and trade-contracting forces*

The record indicates that the forces making for an expansion of world trade more rapid than that of world output have held sway over the trade-contracting forces. Indeed, the growth of trade in absolute terms and relative to output since the Second World War has consistently exceeded the predictions of forecasters.[5] It is therefore appropriate to review briefly the types of influences that have been deemed significant in encouraging (or discouraging) foreign trade.[6]

Probably the most important factor accounting for the surge forward in trade has been the removal of trade barriers as a consequence of multilateral negotiations within GATT, on the one hand, and the formation of free trade areas, customs unions, or other special arrangements (e.g., the Canada-U.S. auto pact), on the other hand. New products have thus been enabled to enter world trade, and the volumes of products already traded have been increased. More efficient organization of production has occurred as increased competition has forced greater specialization of existing production so that potential economies of scale might be realized. Much of the specialization has been of an intra-industry nature, so that cross-flows of products among countries within individual industries have increased—and at a more rapid pace than the increase in industrial production.[7] (In contrast, where tariffs have not been removed but, instead, additional barriers have been erected, trade has flagged. The actual or *de facto* import quotas on labour-intensive commodities, especially textiles and clothing, and agricultural protectionism are the prominent illustrations.)

As tariff barriers on imports have been reduced, nations have emphasized the expansion of exports as a means of strengthening their balances on merchandise account and improving their balances of payments. The measures adopted have taken a variety of forms, ranging from domestic educational programs, aimed at stimulating greater interest in exporting, to more specific export subsidies such as the provision of credit to exporters at below-market rates of interest (which they in turn can pass on to foreign buyers), export insurance, or market surveys or other export promotional services abroad. Subsidies to large firms to locate plants and research and development facilities in particular countries have supported the trend towards

[5]Some countries, such as the United Kingdom and the United States, experienced slower growth rates in their output and international commerce than were predicted for them. But other nations, such as Japan, Italy, and Spain, did much better than the forecasts. See, for example, OECD, *The Growth of Output, 1960–1980*, Geneva, 1970, Chap. 1.
[6]See especially Slater, *World Trade* ..., Chaps. 1, 3, 4, 8, and 9.
[7]For a recent analysis of intra-industry trade, see H. G. Grubel and P. J. Lloyd, "The Empirical Measurement of Intra-Industry Trade," mimeographed, Australian National University, 1970.

greater intra-industry specialization among nations and have increased the international flows of materials, components, and final products.

Concurrently, rising incomes, increased international travel, and improved communications have all contributed to the development of cosmopolitan tastes and hence have been a spur to world trade. Technological advances in the transportation industry—containerization, pelletization, ever-larger ocean tankers, huge jet aircraft—have been assigned some significance in reducing the costs of transport relative to the value of products and in facilitating trade expansion. And they may be of greater importance in the future.

The extension of the operations of corporations beyond their original national boundaries has been an integral part of the augmentation of world production and trade over the past quarter century. International corporations have been in a position to capitalize on the foregoing expansionary forces and also have contributed to their impact. Much of the intra-industry specialization occurring as tariffs have been reduced undoubtedly has been intra-corporate specialization. The giant firms are able to draw resources from a variety of countries, process them in other places, and market them in still other nations. By producing individual materials or components in separate countries, the companies are able to reduce their vulnerability to complete disruption of their world production and distribution programs stemming from possible confiscatory policies of individual national governments. As tastes become more cosmopolitan and the speed with which products can be transported is improved, greater economies of scale in their promotional and other marketing activities are achievable. And as nations provide locational or other subsidies, the firms are able to pick and choose among options to maximize their own advantage.

A first glance at some of the facts might suggest that the international corporation has tended to diminish world trade. For example, the production of these firms beyond the boundaries of their home countries is now approximately double the exports of the major industrial countries.[8] This observation seems consistent with a view held in earlier years that increased factor mobility, particularly capital and skilled management, and the accompanying dissemination of technology would reduce trade by lessening differences among countries in relative factor proportions and technological capabilities.

This position, however, ignores the phenomenon of intra-industry and intra-corporate specialization and diversification mentioned above. The expansion of intra-EEC trade and intra-EFTA trade seems to have been of

[8]Sidney E. Rolfe, "The International Corporation in Perspective," in *The Multinational Corporation in the World Economy: Direct Investment in Perspective*, ed. Sidney E. Rolfe and Walter Damm, New York, Praeger Publishers, 1970, pp. 6–9.

this form.[9] The above position ignores too that the large corporation is a major source of research and development. The steady stream of advanced and differentiated products and processes that emanate from such research and development suggests that, although the establishment of production facilities in other countries may replace exports of some products to these lands, other, newly developed products may more than take their places in trade flows.[10] Product differentiation is now widely recognized as an important feature of international commerce among developed nations.[11]

Moreover, the flow of the original products internationally may not cease because of their production's being undertaken in a country to which the innovating country previously exported. Rather, if the new country is a lower-cost location, the flow of products may now be reversed, going back to the innovating country. This possibility, up to now at least, probably has been most important for products first developed in the United States and subsequently produced in other industrial, but lower-labour-cost, nations.[12]

These factors, then—lower tariffs, increased export subsidies, improved international communication and transportation leading to increasing diversity in consumers' tastes, the expansion of corporations internationally, and the product cycle—have all apparently played a role in causing world trade to grow more rapidly than world output.

This is not to say that no forces have been working in the opposite direction. Certainly, restrictions on labour-intensive manufactured imports, government buy-at-home policies, and the host of other non-tariff barriers that have been tabulated by GATT have obstructed trade flows. Also the balance of payments deficits of the key currency countries, the United Kingdom and the United States, and the implications for world liquidity and the stability of the world monetary system of these deficits have undoubtedly increased uncertainty and probably hindered commodity movements on occasion. But over the past two and one-half decades, these negative factors have been overwhelmed by the positive forces making for faster expansion of world trade.

Then too, although low income elasticities of demand for many types of food, agricultural protectionism on temperate-climate products, improved

[9]See Andrew Schonitz, "The Impact of Trade Blocs on Foreign Direct Investment," *Economic Journal*, 80, Sept. 1970, pp. 724–31.
[10]See Raymond Vernon, "International Investment and International Trade in the Product Cycle," *Quarterly Journal of Economics*, 80, May 1966, pp. 190–207; also Raymond Vernon, ed., *The Technology Factor in International Trade*, National Bureau of Economic Research, New York, Columbia University Press, 1970.
[11]See Richard E. Caves, "Foreign Investment, Trade and Industrial Growth," The Royer Lectures, University of California, Berkeley, Dec. 1–2, 1969.
[12]With regard to the product cycle and developing countries, see the next section.

efficiency in the use of raw materials, and expanded use of synthetics help to account for the growth of trade in primary products being slower than that for manufactures, these factors have not been sufficient to prevent even trade in primary products growing more rapidly than the production of such goods.

*Prospects*

Prospects for the rest of the present decade are far from clear. Even apart from the factors mentioned in the previous paragraph which have tended to dampen world trade, a number of other influences also cloud the picture. Most significant perhaps is the rising protectionist sentiment of labour groups, particularly within the United States. This sentiment shows itself both in attempts to obtain new import quotas on a wide range of products and through encouraging international unions to move towards negotiating world-wide wage contracts, thus reducing or conceivably eliminating the labour-cost advantages of other nations. The increasingly inward-looking view of the European Economic Community and growing nationalism within some developing and developed nations (which could lead to autarkic policies) are part of the present environment. There is also increasing hostility to the behaviour of international corporations pursuing their own interests often without regard to the interests of the individual nations within which they are operating. One view is that measures designed to counter their behaviour may also severely dampen their expansive impact upon world trade.[13] Inflation has become a worldwide problem, and measures taken to counter it have dampened employment, output, and trade.

But despite the fact that these considerations cast a shadow over the world economy, it is probably fair to say that an air of cautious optimism still exists. The forces making for rapid growth of output and trade over the past two decades are expected to prevail.

Some support for this position is to be found in the performance of world commerce during 1970 and 1971. For 1970, the rate of expansion of world production was only a little more than 3 percent, the slowest it had been for twelve years.[14] But in contrast to 1958, when a significant decline in the growth rate of world output was accompanied by a drop in world

[13]The dilemma of whether to let these corporations continue their massive expansion unabated and possibly see them supercede nations as the dominant unit of organization or whether to restrict their development and possibly retard world growth is posed by Stephen Hymer in "United States Investment Abroad," Third Pacific Trade and Development Conference, University of New South Wales, Sydney, Aug. 1970.
[14]This paragraph and the following one rely on GATT, *Press Release,* no. 1076, Feb. 12, 1971.

exports, 1970 witnessed a rise in such shipments by 13 percent in value terms and 7 percent in volume terms (9 percent in volume for the OECD area alone). This increase of export volume of more than double the rate of increase in production also compares fairly well with the average trade-volume expansion for the 1960s of about 8 percent annually. Moreover, "*in relation to world output,* world trade increased more rapidly in 1970 than in any other post-war slowdown."[15]

The performance of the United States was a key factor in world results. The major reason for the slowdown in world production growth was the slowdown in that country. At the same time, American demand for imports rose by 11 percent, whereas in the 1958 slowdown it declined. Other factors seen to be of consequence were the continuing Kennedy Round tariff reductions (which will not be complete until 1972), a revival of world food exports, and the institution of Special Drawing Rights in January of 1970, which provided an increase in the foreign-exchange reserves of countries frequently having balance of payments deficits.

During 1971, world industrial output again lagged badly, but world trade still expanded 7 percent in volume and about 12–13 percent in value.

Projections for 1972 indicate that trade is expected to expand as rapidly as in 1971 or even faster. For 1973 the outlook is even more promising.[16]

Longer-term projections for Canadian trade are quite optimistic. In 1969 the Economic Council of Canada[17] estimated the annual increases in exports and imports between 1967 and 1975 at 10.2 percent and 10.3 percent, respectively. The fastest export growth was anticipated in industrial materials and highly manufactured goods, with little improvement foreseen for grain shipments abroad. Import expansion was expected to be concentrated in highly manufactured products. The merchandise account was projected to have a $1-billion surplus in 1975, whereas invisibles (primarily interest, dividends, and business service charges) would have a deficit of $2–2½ billion, thus necessitating a long-term capital inflow of $1–1½ billion. These projections, however, were published prior to the severe anti-inflationary

---

[15]*Ibid.*, p. 2.

[16]*National Institute Economic Review*, Feb. 1972, pp. 49–50.

There can be no denying, however, that the U.S. balance of payments crisis of 1971 and the subsequent circumstances increased uncertainties about the future course of world production and trade. In December, 1970, the OECD boldly projected that increases in OECD area production to the end of 1980 would average 5.3 percent annually, compared with realized increases of 4.8 percent annually for the 1960s (OECD, *The Growth of Output, 1960–1980: Retrospect, Prospect and Problems of Policy,* Geneva, Dec. 1970, p. 79). But at the end of 1971 they were unwilling to commit themselves on trade projections for longer than six months (OECD, *Economic Outlook,* Geneva, Nov. 1971).

[17]*The Sixth Annual Review: Perspective 1975*, Ottawa, Queen's Printer, 1969, pp. 87–91.

measures of late 1969 and 1970; the resulting drop in imports in 1970; the upward pressure on the Canadian dollar, leading to its release in June of 1970 to find its own level; confirmation of Britain's entry into the EEC; and the realignment of currencies in December, 1971. At present, the longer-term implications of these developments for Canadian trade are difficult to foretell, but they will be the subject of some analysis and comment in subsequent chapters.

Total exports of the developing nations, at least to the mid-1970s, promise to continue growing, but will do so more slowly than shipments abroad by the industrial nations. Rates of increase are projected to be from 4 percent to well over 5 percent.[18] This slower growth stems primarily from the concentration of developing countries upon primary products and industrial materials. Their exports of manufactures are expected to compare quite well with exports of such products by the developed nations, with estimates ranging from 7.5 percent to 9.0 percent per annum.[19]

These projections for manufacturing exports by developing nations are in part based upon a switch in policy over recent years by a number of developing countries—from import substitution to an emphasis upon exporting and exposing their industries to international competition. They also reflect in part, on the one hand, the fact that corporations from all the industrial nations are recognizing the cost advantages of undertaking the labour-intensive portions of their manufacture in the developing nations and exporting back to their homelands and other developed nations and, on the other hand, that the developing nations are aware that the flows of specialized resources to them enable them to utilize previously unexploited comparative advantages in labour-intensive products. The estimates were made, however, prior to an agreement among the developed countries to extend tariff preferences to the developing nations. At the time of writing, it remains to be seen what effect these arrangements will have on trade. In any event, until the industrial countries also reduce or remove their negotiated restraints on exports from the developing countries, the potential flows of such manufactures will be far from fully developed, and the poorer nations' expansion and world trade will be somewhat thwarted.

It should be noted that new flows of labour-intensive products to developed lands would not be simply a reversal of previous shipments in the opposite direction. Rather they would be largely net increments to world trade. Previously they were probably not imported because the developing

[18]See Alfred Maizels, *Exports and Economic Growth of Developing Countries*, Cambridge, University Press, 1968, Table 5.10, p. 147; and UNCTAD, *Trade Prospects and Capital Needs of Developing Countries*, New York, United Nations, 1969, p. 19.
[19]*Ibid.*

countries either were supplying themselves (as with clothing and other tex-tiles) or had little demand for them (as with electronic components). Notice, too, that the flow of products would not all be one way. The developed nations would be able to increase their shipments to the developing nations in the form of machinery and equipment and other sophisticated products demanded as incomes rise.

Another potential area for great expansion in trade is, of course, between the West and the Communist bloc. Some growth has occurred in recent years, particularly between Eastern and Western Europe, but scope remains for much further development of these trade relations.

# 4. A First Approximation to Free Trade Alternatives for Canada

As a prelude to the analysis that will follow in subsequent chapters concerning the impact of various free trade alternatives on Canadian production and trade, this chapter offers an initial assessment of five such possibilities. The emphasis here is on short-term or static results, although some dynamic considerations are introduced towards the end of the chapter. The results give only rough orders of magnitude concerning the effect on the major components and direction of Canadian trade, indicating what issues would need to be carefully considered by Canada if one of these alternatives were to become a reality. By putting numbers, albeit rough ones, on the outcomes of the various alternatives, the *relative* sizes of the resulting changes in trade flows—and the consequences for particular Canadian sectors or industries and, more generally, for wages and/or the exchange rate—can be more easily visualized.

The five free trade associations considered are as follows:
(1) Canada and the United States;
(2) Canada, the United States, and the European Free Trade Asociation (EFTA) countries;
(3) Canada, the United States, and the three developed Pacific countries—Japan, Australia, and New Zealand;
(4) Number 3 without the United States;
(5) Number 3 and EFTA and the European Economic Community (EEC).

A few comments should be made as to why these particular configurations were selected for discussion. The rationale for including the first one hardly needs mention. The exceptionally high proportion of Canadian trade that is conducted with the United States and the extensive ties between Canadian and American industry via the high proportion of Canadian resources and manufacturing controlled by American parent firms warrant consideration of this relationship. Also, although American initiatives towards greater liberation of world trade have, since the Kennedy Round, been limited and although strong protectionist sentiment prevails in many quarters in the United States, there are some indications that Americans might permit themselves to be persuaded of the benefits of a Canada-U.S.

free trade agreement. U.S. interest in Canadian natural gas, oil, and (whether implicitly or explicitly stated) water resources suggests that this scheme might appeal to Washington. In any event, a Canada-U.S. free trade arrangement seems a logical place—at least from a purely economic viewpoint—to commence discussion of free trade alternatives of interest to Canada.

The second proposal, a Canada-U.S.-EFTA arrangement, has received considerable attention in recent years as an alternative to entry into the EEC for the United Kingdom and its EFTA associates. This proposal was still a possibility when the first draft of this chapter was being prepared. Now that Britain and some other EFTA countries are joining the EEC, this alternative is really no longer relevant. Still, it seems worthwhile to examine the impact of such an arrangement upon Canada if only to compare the results with the remaining alternatives Canada could reasonably consider.

In the third alternative a Pacific orientation is substituted for the foregoing Atlantic one. This is a possibility that must be taken seriously, for a variety of reasons. Consider first the position of Japan. As the world's third-strongest industrial nation, it cannot be ignored in any future discussion of new free trade blocs among developed nations. The need is paramount for a strong nation in Asia, favourably disposed to the West, and capable of assuming a growing responsibility for aid to, and investment in, the less developed nations of the Pacific. The Japanese have chosen economic rather than military methods of assuring themselves of supplies of raw materials and markets for their products, and this choice must receive the continuing support of the West. Also, Japan provides a large market for the products of Western nations, not only for raw materials but also for semi-processed and highly manufactured goods.[1] Finally, the Japanese have shown much interest in free trade (admittedly without wishing to include agriculture—of which more will be said later) and make no apologies about wanting to be included in any free trade discussions under way. One method they have adopted in their desire to ensure such inclusion is the initiation of talks, among professional specialists from various countries, on subjects related to their own international trading interests.[2]

Australia and New Zealand, like Canada, are developed nations lacking

[1]See G. C. Allen, *Japan's Place in Trade Strategy: Larger Role in Pacific Region*, London, Atlantic Trade Study, 1969.
[2]See Kiyoshi Kojima, ed., *Pacific Trade and Development: Papers and Proceedings of a Conference held by the Japan Economic Research Centre*, Jan. 1968, Tokyo, Japan Economic Research Centre, 1968; and *Pacific Trade and Development II: Papers and Proceedings of a Conference held by The East-West Centre*, Honolulu, Jan. 1969, Tokyo, Japan Economic Research Centre, 1969.

free access to larger markets. With the British joining the EEC, possibly some form of associate status might eventually be worked out for them. But this seems far in the future, and their economies are complementary with the Japanese economy and their trade with that nation is growing rapidly.

The fourth proposal—a free trade area in which only Canada, Australia, New Zealand, and Japan would participate initially—may become of greater relevance than first thoughts would suggest. If Britain enters the EEC and if the United States continues to register little or no interest in regional trade arrangements regardless of their open-ended nature, such an alternative might be the only vehicle by means of which these countries could participate in a widening of their markets unrestricted by tariffs and quotas. From Canada's viewpoint, there may be more in favour of such a scheme than simply access to a wider market.

The great trust Canada has placed in the United States as a market and a source of supply has a number of important implications; one of these relates to Canadian economic stability. The Canadian business cycle, Canadian exports to the United States, and the U.S. business cycle all tend to coincide with one another. In contrast, British purchases from Canada do not bear a consistent relationship to Canadian cyclical activity, and purchases by third countries sometimes move in a fashion counter to the Canadian cycle.[3]

This topic admittedly needs more empirical investigation. In any event, what is known to date suggests that, although Canada's heavy dependence upon the United States means that Canadians share intimately in the benefits of American prosperity, it also implies greater problems of cyclical stabilization than if the country's export markets were more diversified.

In addition, almost complete reliance upon the United States as a market and source of supply makes Canada particularly vulnerable to strikes and other labour problems interrupting production in the United States. A greater diversification of Canadian trade would reduce the extent of the shock from such disturbances in the United States, and there would be a greater probability that random disturbances abroad would to some degree cancel one another out in terms of their impact upon the Canadian economy. Greater diversification would also help to improve Canada's bargaining position in trade negotiations with the United States.

The fifth and final proposal—encompassing the EEC, EFTA, the Pacific developed countries, the United States, and Canada—is, under present circumstances, clearly far in the future. Such an arrangement, coupled with

[3]T. Russell Robinson, *Foreign Trade and Economic Stability,* Staff Study no. 5 of the Royal Commission on Taxation, Ottawa, Queen's Printer, 1967, pp. 108–10.

free imports from the less developed nations, is little more than a goal towards which the developed countries might be working. Still, because it is a desirable possibility, it is of some value to note the impact of this broader free trade alternative upon Canadian trade, both in an absolute sense and relative to the other, less-encompassing proposals.

*Approach*

A variety of approaches have been employed to estimate the static effects of discriminatory tariff reductions on trade flows.[4] No one of them is completely satisfactory, particularly with respect to certain problems. For example, there is the question of possible complementarity among some products in a category concurrent with substitutability among the remaining products in that category. Then again, there are problems raised by product differentiation among commodities coming from several countries that are classified into a single product group. And difficulties exist regarding the possibilities of tariff concessions that would permit products to be exported for the first time. A little more comment on these questions will be given shortly.

The approach used in this study is based upon that employed in an earlier paper,[5] which is in turn an adaptation of the Balassa-Kreinin method.[6]

Trade-creation effects (increases in existing trade among member nations resulting from the elimination of tariffs among them) are estimated using relative price elasticities of demand for imports. Trade-diversion effects (the amounts by which imports formerly from outside a particular free trade area will now emanate from other nations within the area as a consequence of tariff removal among them) are derived by using an elasticity of substitution between alternate sources of imports.

The basic equation from which the trade-creation effects were estimated

---

[4]See, for example, Robert M. Stern, "The U.S. Tariff and the Efficiency of the U.S. Economy," *American Economic Review*, 54, May 1964, pp. 459–70; Bela Balassa and M. Kreinin, "Trade Liberalization under the 'Kennedy Round': The Static Effects," *Review of Economics and Statistics*, 49, May 1967, pp. 125–37; L. Krause, *European Economic Integration and the United States,* Washington, Brookings Institution, 1968, Chap. 2 (his approach is adopted from H. G. Johnson, "The International Competitive Position of the United States and the Balance of Payments Prospect for 1968," *Review of Economics and Statistics*, 46, Feb. 1964, p. 24); and Paul S. Armington, "The Geographic Pattern of Trade and Effects of Price Changes," *International Monetary Trend*, Staff Papers, 16, July 1969, pp. 179–201.
[5]B. W. Wilkinson, "A Re-estimation of the Effects of the Formation of a Pacific Area Trade Agreement," *Pacific Trade and Development*, 2, pp. 53–101.
[6]Balassa and Kreinin, "Trade Liberalization ..."

is the common one: $\Delta M_{ij} = M_{ij} \cdot E_i \cdot t_i/(1 + t_i)$, where $M$ is the value of imports, $E$ the importing country's relative price elasticity of demand for imports, $t$ the *ad valorem* tariff rate, $i$ the commodity group, and $j$ the country source of imports.

The equation in this form assumes that the supply of exports from each country for each commodity is perfectly elastic, so that prices of imports to domestic buyers are lowered by the full amount of the tariff reduction. Although a simple adjustment can be made to such an equation to allow for some increase in the supplying country's price when tariffs are reduced, the supposition of infinitely elastic supply has been retained in this study. The rationale for doing so with respect to each participating country is provided in Appendix A to this chapter.

The *initial* import-price elasticities of demand used for each country included in our computations are shown in Table I. The elasticities for the United States are the Ball-Marwah estimates.[7] Those for each of the remaining countries were derived from the American ones following the reasoning employed by Balassa and Kreinin.[8]

These elasticities are for each country's imports from the entire world in the commodity group concerned. The usual assumption made in estimating such elasticities econometrically is that imports from each country in any one commodity group are perfect substitutes for one another. Under such assumptions, however, combined with the suppositions of perfectly elastic export supplies by free trade partners, as well as of constant quantities supplied by nations outside the free trade area, the import-demand elasticity of any one free trade partner facing a supplier nation in the free trade area would be the total elasticity divided by the supplier nation's proportion of the total market. In other words, even if it is assumed that the world consists only of those countries indicated in Table I, for any free trade area comprising less than all these nations, the actual elasticities of import demand by participating countries from one another should be greater than those shown in the table.[9] A further difficulty is that the assumption of

---

[7]R. J. Ball and K. Marwah, "The U.S. Demand for Imports, 1948–1958," *Review of Economics and Statistics*, 44, Nov. 1962, pp. 394–401.

[8]Balassa and Kreinin, "Trade Liberalization ..."

[9]H. G. Johnson has pointed out that, if the items in any commodity group were a bundle of complements whose demand were a function of the average price of the bundle, it would be appropriate to use the demand elasticity for imports from the world in estimating trade creation within the free trade area. That is, "a reduction in the price of the supply from one source, due to devaluation or preferential tariff reduction, will reduce the average price of the bundle by the proportional price reduction of the component multiplied by the share of the component in the total. If we then multiply the average price reduction by the elasticity of demand for the component (overall elasticity divided by component share) we arrive back at the overall elasticity multiplied

TABLE I

ASSUMED PRICE ELASTICITY OF DEMAND FOR IMPORTS (all negative)

| Country | Commodity division | | | | | Percentage of United States' elasticity |
|---|---|---|---|---|---|---|
| | 1 | 2 | 3 | 4 | 5 | |
| United States | 0.34 | 1.87 | 0.26 | 1.38 | 3.50 | 100 |
| Canada, Australia, and New Zealand | 0.17 | 0.94 | 0.13 | 0.69 | 1.75 | 50 |
| Britain | 0.22 | 1.21 | 0.17 | 0.90 | 2.28 | 65 |
| EFTA except Britain | 0.19 | 1.02 | 0.14 | 0.76 | 1.93 | 55 |
| EEC and Japan | 0.26 | 1.40 | 0.20 | 1.04 | 2.63 | 75 |

Source: See text.

homogeneity in estimating trade creation makes it difficult to explain why we have nations regularly importing and exporting products in a single group, and it is also inconsistent with the assumption of imperfect substitutability used in estimating trade diversion on the basis of an elasticity of substitution.

There is no easy solution to these problems. Certainly, a more realistic assumption is that extensive, but imperfect, substitutability exists among products in any one group coming from different countries and between these goods and domestic import-competing production.[10] Then, of course, there are separate demand curves for imports from each country. The price elasticity of any one of these curves probably would be such that the rise in imports from free trade partners would be in between that obtained by simply applying an elasticity of demand for imports from the world to imports from the partner, on the one hand, and that occurring if perfect substitutability prevailed, on the other hand.

---

by the proportional price reduction of the component as the correct measure of the trade-creating increase in demand for the supply from the component."

He has also observed, however, that such an assumption of complementarity contradicts the supposition employed when estimating trade diversion—that is, that there is imperfect substitution among the commodities from different countries within any one commodity group. Commentary by H. G. Johnson on the paper by B. W. Wilkinson, "A Re-estimation ...," pp. 100–1.

[10] A majority of the highly manufactured goods traded internationally, even though included in the same commodity group, are imperfect substitutes one for another and for domestic import-competing production. The exceptions would be items such as textiles and some basic clothing. Even among raw materials, product differences arise. Crude ores, for example, may vary in quality; petroleum may vary in sulphur content or specific gravity, and so on. Where the assumption is least applicable is for refined metals or other materials adhering to well-recognized grading standards. Generally, however, the tariffs on such products are not high, and sensitivity to tariff reductions tends to be low, so that in any event the changes in the flows of these products do not comprise a very large proportion of the total trade-flow changes stemming from free trade. As a broad assumption, imperfect substitutability seems to be a reasonable one.

If an assumption of imperfect substitutability is accepted, then what are needed are estimates of import-price elasticities for each commodity division for each nation from each of its partners in free trade arrangements. Ideally, the income and substitution portions of demand elasticity for imports from any one partner nation in any commodity should be identified, and the substitution part should be subdivided into a series consisting of, first, substitutions between these imports and domestic production and, second, substitutions between them and products from foreign competitors outside the free trade area. After allowing for the income effect, the former substitution would reflect trade creation and the latter would reflect trade diversion.[11]

Such detailed empirical information is simply not available. Even price elasticities for imports of particular commodity groups from particular countries are often hard to come by, and, if available, they frequently vary so widely from study to study as to be only of broad guidance to the researcher attempting to use them.[12] A new set of "guestimates" would be necessary.

Rather than making these new guesses directly, the following procedure was adopted. The estimates of elasticities of demand for imports from the world in Table I were used to provide an initial approximation to trade creation effects.[13] Then, on the assumption that, with close but imperfect

[11]As H. G. Johnson has pointed out in his commentary on Wilkinson's "A Re-estimation ..."

[12]For example, two recent studies examine price elasticities of demand for Canadian exports to the United States for a number of major Canadian exports. A sample of the diversity in results is as follows:

|  | Detomasi (1948–65) | Officer and Hurtubise (1953–65) | |
|---|---|---|---|
|  |  | Least squares | Hilbeth Lu |
| Newsprint | − 0.55 to − 0.81* | −1.58 | −2.45 |
| Woodpulp | −12.05 to −66.81* | −0.62 | −0.83 |
| Iron ore | − 3.04 to −34.77* | −2.04 | −2.90 |
| Aluminum | −22.53 to −82.42* | −1.28 | −0.91 |

*These are the range of values that could occur as the elasticity of supply of each commodity from all other sources than Canada varies between 0.1 and 5.0.
Sources: D. Detomasi, "The Elasticity of Demand for Canadian Exports to the United States," *Canadian Journal of Economics,* 2, Aug. 1969, pp. 416–26; L. H. Officer and J. R. Hurtubise, "Price Effects of the Kennedy Round on Canadian Trade," *Review of Economics and Statistics,* 51, Aug. 1969, pp. 320–33.
[13]This is a pretty unsatisfactory way of proceeding because we are using estimates of import elasticities of demand derived under assumptions of either perfect substitutability or perfect complementarity in a situation where imperfect substitutability has been assumed. At best it can be argued that this technique provides initial figures comparable with earlier studies.

substitutability,[14] the total trade creation would be somewhat greater than the results of the foregoing computations indicate, but less than if perfect substitutability prevailed, an extra trade-creation effect was allowed for. This was done by computing what the maximum additional potential increment in the imports of each country in each commodity division would have been had its tariff reduction occurred vis-à-vis the whole world, rather than just the free trade partner, and assuming that the above import elasticities were applicable and that perfect homogeneity occurred This increment was then reduced by multiplying it by the share of the total imports in that commodity division that were supplied to that country by its free trade partner prior to free trade, thus arriving at the additional trade-creation effect.

In the numerical results of the computations, the initial or usual type of trade-creation effects and what we have called the extra trade-creation effects are presented separately, so that the reader can either include or leave out the extra effects as he sees fit.

For the extra trade-creation effects (and the trade-diversion effects), world trade was deemed to be trade among Canada, the United States, EFTA, EEC, Japan, Australia, and New Zealand—that is to say, most of the major developed countries of the Western world.[15] (Such trade covers between 85 percent and 90 percent of all Canadian exports and imports, respectively.) Hence, when the free trade area is deemed to include all these countries, no extra trade-creation effects enter the picture. This seems a reasonable approach because almost all the trade of the foregoing countries other than with one another may be divided into two categories: with Communist countries and with the less-developed-world countries. Trade with the former countries generally involves state-trading and is unlikely to be affected much by free trade arrangements. As for trade with the developing countries, probably any new free trade arrangements among the developed countries would include some extension of unilateral preferences to at least some of them. A wide variety of possible arrangements might be made. Rather than speculating about such matters, however, and introducing their effects into our initial estimates of trade creation and trade diversion for each free trade alternative, we make a separate estimate of the increases in Canadian imports and exports that

[14]An alternate assumption is that within each commodity group there are some goods that are perfect substitutes for imports, both as between domestic goods and those from within the free trade area and as between goods from the free trade area and those outside it. The remaining goods are independent (essentially non-substitutable) between these two groups.

[15]Israel and South Africa have been ignored in this classification and are therefore included with the less developed nations.

might occur if preferences were granted to all developing countries. This estimate is presented after the other empirical results in this chapter.

For trade diversion, an elasticity of substitution of −2 was used for all nations and commodity groups. Generally speaking, this is a conservative figure compared with empirically derived estimates for a number of the participating countries.[16]

Once the total diversion effect was prepared for each commodity group in a single nation's imports, it was then allocated among the free trade partner countries according to the shares of these nations, by commodity group, in the imports of the country under consideration prior to the free trade arrangement.

Five major commodity divisions were used: crude foodstuffs, processed foodstuffs and feed, crude materials, semi-manufactured non-foodstuffs, and finished manufactures and chemicals. Within these five divisions, 125 SITC groups were distinguished—some at the four-digit level where such detail was warranted. The United Nations import statistics for 1966 were employed.

Import-duty rates were the GATT and British preferential ones adjusted for the Kennedy Round. Details on the computation of these rates, other procedures used in the estimation of the static effects, and a listing of the SITC categories distinguished are provided in Appendix A.

In general, where some arbitrary decisions were necessary in preparing the estimates, they were made so as to indicate the most unfavourable effects on Canadian trade patterns (or something close to that) of the various free trade alternatives. Therefore, these estimates indicate the *maximum* extent to which positive, dynamic changes would have to "offset" these static effects, or the *maximum* devaluation that would be necessary if Canada were to avoid downward pressure on wages and/or increased capital inflows. In cases where the trade balance shows a net improvement, the adjustment mechanism may have to operate in the opposite direction.

It must be emphasized that our interest is in indicating the relative magni-

---

[16]For example, see H. B. Junz and R. R. Rhomberg, "Prices and Export Performances of Industrial Countries, 1953–1963," *IMF Staff Papers*, July 1965, Table, p. 240.

The formula employed was: $r = 2etq_fq_w/[q_w (2 + t - et) + q_f (2 + t + et)]$ where the world price of a commodity group exclusive of the tariff is unity, $t$ is the *ad valorem* tariff, $p_f$ is the pre-free trade domestic price of imports from partner countries inclusive of the tariff (i.e., $p_f = 1 + t$), $p_w$ is the pre- and post-free trade domestic price of imports from the rest of the world inclusive of the tariff, $q_f$ is the quantity and value of imports of a nation from free trade partners, $q_w$ is the quantity and value of pre-free trade imports from non-member countries, and $r$ is the amount by which the quantity of imports from free trade partners increases and from the rest of the world decreases owing to a free trade arrangement. For a derivation of the formula, see B. W. Wilkinson, "A Re-estimation ..."

tudes of the net trade changes for the different free trade alternatives and in highlighting the main issues involved in free trade. Therefore, while the absolute size of our results would be greater had 1971 trade flows been employed, the ranking of the five alternatives would not likely be altered.[17]

*Static trade-creation and trade-diversion effects*

Table II provides a summary of the static merchandise-trade effects of the five free trade alternatives under consideration in this chapter. All commodities are included in the estimates, including both agricultural goods and fuels. A common argument is that these latter two product groups should be excluded because world trade in such commodities is so greatly influenced by non-tariff restrictions such as domestic support programs and import quotas.[18] However, trade in many manufactured commodities is also subject to non-tariff restrictions, ranging from quotas and "buy national" policies to research and development subsidies and subsidized export-credit arrangements. Moreover, one might argue, as Ronald Wonnacott[19] has done, that an elasticities approach is inappropriate for highly manufactured goods when one or more of the participants hopes to realize large, dynamic benefits from trade liberalization in the form of economies of scale in production (and possibly marketing), greater efficiency from increased competitiveness, and so on. This would leave only trade in crude materials and semi-processed commodities other than fuels as appropriate candidates for estimation by the elasticities method. One could, of course, carry one's scepticism of the approach even further by pointing out that many international movements of crude materials and semi-manufactured products are regulated largely by long-term contracts and parent-subsidiary ties, so that an elasticities approach may often be inappropriate for these goods as well, at least in the short term.

In brief, then, the appropriateness of the elasticities method of estimating trade increments when tariffs are removed is clearly one of degree, and differences of opinion are possible as to the relevance of the results in particular product groups. The question is primarily one of where to draw the line. Our approach has been to exclude no commodity groups initially and then to modify or elaborate on the calculations with further quantitative and qualitative discussion.

[17]See the final section of this chapter.
[18]See Balassa and Kreinin, "Trade Liberalization ..."
[19]"Trade Arrangements Among Industrial Countries: Effects on Canada," in *Studies in Trade Liberalization*, ed. Bela Balassa, Baltimore, Johns Hopkins Press, 1967, pp. 53–5.

TABLE II

ESTIMATES OF TRADE CREATION FROM THE STATIC EFFECTS OF VARIOUS FREE TRADE
ALTERNATIVES BASED ON 1966 CANADIAN TRADE (million U.S. dollars)

| | Free trade partners | | | | |
|---|---|---|---|---|---|
| | USA (1) | USA and EFTA (2) | USA and J/A/NZ[a] (3) | J/A/NZ[a] (4) | USA, EFTA, EEC, J/A/NZ[a] (5) |
| *Canadian imports* | | | | | |
| (1)   (a) First approximation | 706 | 777 | 758 | 51 | 915 |
| (2)   (b) Extra effect | 129 | 105 | 112 | 42 | — |
| (3)     Total | 835 | 883 | 870 | 93 | 915 |
| (4)   Trade diversion | 185 | 114 | 191 | 65 | — |
| *Canadian exports* | | | | | |
| (5)   (a) First approximation | 340 | 360 | 378 | 38 | 439 |
| (6)   (b) Extra effect | 301 | 226 | 234 | 20 | — |
| (7)     Total | 641 | 586 | 612 | 58 | 439 |
| (8)   Trade diversion | 237 | 214 | 182 | 76 | — |
| (9)     Total increase | 878 | 800 | 794 | 132 | 439 |
| *Net change in trade balance* | | | | | |
| (10) Including extra trade- creation effects | +43 | −82 | −76 | +39 | −476 |
| (11) Excluding extra trade- creation effects | −129 | −202 | −198 | +61 | −476 |
| *Percentage increase in total* (including extra trade- creation effects) | | | | | |
| (12) (a) Imports | 9.1 | 9.6 | 9.5 | 1.0 | 10.0 |
| (13) (b) Exports | 9.4 | 8.6 | 8.6 | 1.4 | 4.7 |

[a]Japan, Australia, New Zealand.
Source: See text.

Table II is largely self-explanatory, but it may be worthwhile to follow through in detail the calculations for one of the free trade alternatives and then to highlight some of the more interesting conclusions for the other alternatives. Consider column 1, giving the changes in trade flows from a Canada-U.S. arrangement. If we look only at the first approximation of trade-creation effects (rows 1 and 5), it appears that Canada would experience an adverse alteration in its trade balance of nearly U.S.$370 million. This effect would be created because Canadian imports are concentrated in highly manufactured goods, and these goods are quite sensitive to tariff-rate changes and are subject to tariff rates that tend to be fairly high. Canadian exports, in contrast, are largely crude materials, and these materials are not very responsive to tariff changes and already face low foreign tariffs.

Considering the extra trade-creation effects alone (rows 2 and 6), it seems that Canada would gain more on the merchandise account than it would lose. This consequence derives from the fact that Canada is a supplier of about 25 percent of U.S. imports and thus would benefit substantially from the extra effect. Yet because 70 to 75 percent of Canadian imports are already from the United States, the extra effect on Canadian imports would not be great, and most of the impact of such an agreement on imports would already have been picked up in the initial effects.

Counting both the initial and extra trade-creation effects (rows 3 and 7), Canada's balance of trade would deteriorate by nearly U.S.$200 million.

Trade diversion, however, results in Canadian exports increasing by about U.S.$240 million (row 8). That is, Canada replaces other countries as a supplier of the American market by this amount. The diversion of Canadian purchases from non-member countries to the United States, amounting to U.S.$185 million (row 4), would not alter Canada's balance on merchandise trade with the total world. Only the source of imports would be changed. The net effect of trade diversion, then, is to improve the trade balance by the amount of the expansion in exports, or U.S.$240 million.

In total, the net change in the Canadian trade balance of a Canada-U.S. agreement would be an improvement approaching U.S.$45 million (row 10) if all trade-creation and trade-diversion effects are counted. If only the first approximations to trade-creation estimates are included in the totals, a deficit of nearly U.S.$130 million would ensue. Either way, the *net* changes are modest. Increases in the gross flows of total Canadian imports and exports would also be relatively small: the proportional growth would be, respectively, 9.1 percent and 9.4 percent, which is approximately the average rate of trade expansion that was measured for all industrial countries (and Canadian exports too) between 1960 and 1969 and less than the growth of Canadian imports over the same period.

Such an agreement would increase the concentration of Canadian trade with the United States by a further 7 or 8 percentage points, so that, in terms of the 1969 trade directions, 80 percent of all Canada's foreign trade would be with that country.

Under the second and third free trade possibilities (that is, Canada, the United States, and EFTA, on the one hand, and Canada, the United States, and Japan/Australia/New Zealand, on the other), the magnitudes involved are quite similar, reflecting the comparable size of Canadian trade with EFTA and with Japan/Australia/New Zealand. The deficit Canada would experience from such country groupings might fluctuate between about

U.S.$75 million and U.S.$200 million, depending upon whether the extra trade-creation effects were realized. The less favourable results of these possible arrangements compared with a simple Canada-U.S. agreement spring from the reduction in Canadian exports that would occur. Because more countries would be able to export duty-free to the United States, Canada would stand to gain less on exports to the American market, from either the extra trade-creation effects or the trade-diversion effects, and would not make up the loss through offsetting new exports to the added free trade partners, in whose markets Canada has but a small share.

The most unfavourable free trade arrangement, from the viewpoint of its impact upon the Canadian balance of merchandise trade, is the one comprising Canada, the United States, EFTA, EEC, and Japan/Australia/New Zealand (column 5). Under such an agreement, Canadian imports would rise by over U.S.$900 million, but exports would not keep pace—at least not under the static assumptions of this portion of the analysis. Because it was assumed that trade with nations outside this grouping would be little affected by free trade arrangements among them, Canada would not gain any expansion of exports from the extra trade-creation or trade-diversion effects. The estimated deficit, then, would approach U.S.$480 million. Gross imports would be increased by 10 percent, but exports would be only 4.7 percent greater than without this free trade arrangement.

The final alternative—free trade among Canada, Australia, New Zealand, and Japan (column 4)—would initially cover no more than 3.3 percent of Canadian imports and 5.4 percent of Canadian exports.[20] Consequently, as one would expect, the absolute and percentage increases in trade are tiny indeed. Such small results dramatize, far better than do the other results in Table II, a previously mentioned limitation of this static elasticities method of estimating trade growth from tariff removal—that is, its failure to give any indication of the magnitude of new trade in commodities not previously exchanged. The size, diversity, and technologically advanced nature of the Japanese economy suggest that the possible substitution of Japan for the United States as a source of many highly manufactured imports is underestimated by our above procedure. In other words, both trade creation and trade diversion in Canadian imports under this alternative appear much understated. Canada, in turn, might be expected to find itself able to export new products to Japan as well, not to mention possibilities with respect to Australia and New Zealand.

[20]These numbers are for 1966. For 1969, the numbers would be 3.4 and 6.9 percent, respectively, reflecting the continued rapid growth of trade with these nations, particularly Japan.

TABLE III

CHANGES IN 1966 CANADIAN TRADE UNDER VARIOUS FREE TRADE ALTERNATIVES
ASSUMING THREE DIFFERENT SETS OF IMPORT-PRICE ELASTICITIES OF DEMAND

| | | Free trade partners | | | |
|---|---|---|---|---|---|
| | USA (1) | USA and EFTA (2) | USA and J/A/NZ[a] (3) | J/A/NZ[a] (4) | USA EFTA, EEC, J/A/NZ[a] (5) |
| *Import-price elasticities* | | | | | |
| Low:[b]  (a) Percentage rise in imports | 4.6 | 4.8 | 4.8 | .5 | 5.0 |
| (b) Percentage rise in exports | 6.0 | 5.4 | 5.2 | 1.1 | 2.4 |
| (c) Net change in trade balance (million U.S. dollars) | +150 | +66 | +55 | +58 | −238 |
| Medium: (a) Percentage rise in imports | 9.1 | 9.6 | 9.5 | 1.0 | 10.0 |
| (b) Percentage rise in exports | 9.4 | 8.5 | 8.5 | 1.4 | 4.7 |
| (c) Net change in trade balance (million U.S. dollars) | +43 | −82 | −75 | +39 | −476 |
| High:[c]  (a) Percentage rise in imports | 18.2 | 19.2 | 19.0 | 2.0 | 20.0 |
| (b) Percentage rise in exports | 16.3 | 14.8 | 15.0 | 2.1 | 9.4 |
| (c) Net change in trade balance (million U.S. dollars) | −152 | −380 | −332 | +6 | −952 |

[a]Japan, Australia, New Zealand.
[b]Elasticities assumed to be one-half the medium elasticities.
[c]Elasticities assumed to be double the medium elasticities.
Source: See text.

*Alternative assumptions*

Before examining the behaviour of individual commodity divisions and groups under our five free trade proposals, we will present a brief summary of the effects upon Canadian trade flows and balances of altering elasticity assumptions. Table III shows the Canadian net merchandise trade balances under three different assumptions for each country's (or group of countries') price elasticities of demand for imports. The medium elasticity results are reproduced from Table II. The low and high results assume that elasticities for the participating countries are one-half of, and double, the medium elasticities, respectively. The extra trade-creation effects are included in each case, and the elasticity of substitution is left at −2. With a low sensitivity of trade to tariff changes, the Canadian merchandise balance is more favourable. These results are much as might have been expected, given that Canadian exports are clustered in the crude materials and semi-processed-product categories, which are relatively insensitive to tariff changes (and upon which tariffs are already quite low), whereas imports are mostly high-tariff, highly manufactured goods, which exhibit the greatest responsiveness to tariff changes of any of the commodity groups.

If the elasticity of substitution were −1, the favourable trade-diversion effects on Canadian exports—where these exist—would be cut approximately in half. Although the details are not presented, the reader may easily verify, by reference to Table II, that this would mean a worsening in the Canadian trade balance of about $100 million in any one of the first three free trade alternatives and of about $40 million in the fourth alternative and no change in the fifth. Alternately, an elasticity of substitution greater than −2 (absolutely) would make the Canadian trade balance more favourable than we show, except again in the fifth alternative, where it would remain unaltered.

*Trade effects by commodity group*

In considering the commodity composition of the changes in trade flows resulting from tariff elimination, we revert to our original assumptions of an elasticity of substitution of −2 and what we have referred to in Table III as medium import-price elasticities. The results for the five major commodity divisions are shown in Table IV.

The overwhelming source of import expansion is in the finished-manufactures and chemicals category. The major *import*-growth subsectors in order of estimated pace of increase are as follows: electrical machinery and apparatus; chemicals of all types; textile fabrics and clothing; and professional, scientific, and controlling instruments and apparatus. To give some idea of magnitudes, a free trade arrangement with the United States alone would result in additional non-electrical-machinery imports of U.S.$250 million. (Counting the diversion from other supply sources, inflows of such products from the United States would swell by U.S.$300 million.) For electrical machinery the increase would be U.S.$115 million; for chemicals, $95 million; for textiles, $90 million; and for instruments, $60 million.

These same relative orders of magnitude are observed when the EFTA nations are added to the free trade area. However, once Japan is intro-

TABLE IV

ESTIMATES OF STATIC EFFECTS OF VARIOUS FREE TRADE ALTERNATIVES ON 1966 CANADIAN TRADE, BY MAJOR COMMODITY DIVISION[a,b] (million U.S. dollars)

| | Free trade partners | | | | |
| --- | --- | --- | --- | --- | --- |
| | USA (1) | USA and EFTA (2) | USA and J/A/NZ[c] (3) | J/A/NZ[c] (4) | USA, EFTA, EEC, J/A/NZ[c] (5) |
| *Imports* | | | | | |
| Crude foodstuffs and feed | 3 | 3 | 3 | _[d] | 4 |
| Processed foodstuffs and feed | 5 | 8 | 5 | 3 | 10 |
| Crude materials | 1 | 1 | 1 | _[d] | 1 |
| Semi-manufactures | 21 | 21 | 21 | 2 | 22 |
| Finished manufactures and chemicals | 806 | 850 | 869 | 89 | 879 |
| Total imports | 835 | 882 | 869 | 93 | 915 |
| *Exports*[e] | | | | | |
| Crude foodstuffs and feed | 12 | 41 | 14 | 39 | 21 |
| Processed foodstuffs and feed | 103 | 87 | 82 | 5 | 50 |
| Crude materials | 19 | 17 | 18 | 10 | 12 |
| Semi-manufactures | 132 | 130 | 127 | 19 | 79 |
| Finished manufactures and chemicals | 612 | 525 | 554 | 60 | 277 |
| Total exports | 878 | 800 | 794 | 132 | 439 |
| *Net changes in trade balance* | | | | | |
| Crude foodstuffs and feed | +9 | +38 | +11 | +38 | +17 |
| Processed foodstuffs and feed | +98 | +79 | +77 | +3 | +41 |
| Crude materials | +19 | +17 | +18 | +10 | +11 |
| Semi-manufactures | +111 | +109 | +106 | +17 | +56 |
| Finished manufactures and chemicals | −194 | −325 | −285 | −29 | −602 |
| Net change in trade balance | +43 | −82 | −76 | +39 | −476 |

[a]Medium import-price elasticities and elasticity of substitution of −2 are assumed.
[b]Totals may not add because of rounding.
[c]Japan, Australia, New Zealand.
[d]Less than 0.5.
[e]Includes trade-creation and trade-diversion effects.
Source: See text.

duced, as in the third, fourth, and fifth alternatives, textiles and clothing would replace chemicals and possibly some of the other commodities in order of importance.

Not too much emphasis should be placed upon the individual figures presented for product groups within any one of the five main divisions. Such calculations can do little more than alert us to the main product groups in which domestic adjustments in the face of free trade would have to be substantial. The most notable example of this indicated need for adjustment is the textiles and clothing group. The elasticity estimate used here, omitting as it does all reference to actual or *de facto* import or export quotas, understates the increment in imports of such products that would occur under completely unhindered trade. Our method suggests that inflows of such goods from Japan, in the event of a Canada-Japan/Australia/New Zealand free trade arrangement, would be augmented by no more than U.S.$40 million. We need only compare this figure with 1966 Canadian shipments of Can.$2,821 billion produced under an umbrella of negotiated Japanese (and developing-nation) export restrictions to realize that it is very much on the low side. Similar comments would apply to some electronic parts and equipment, although the magnitudes involved would not be as large.

As for exports, increments in the finished-manufactures and chemicals division again dominate the results, with machinery (both electrical and non-electrical) and chemicals the leading product groups. In contrast to imports, however, increases in semi-manufactured goods and processed foodstuffs are also shown as significant. Non-ferrous metals, especially copper, nickel, and aluminum, account for three-quarters of the indicated expansion of semi-manufactured exports. Fish, tobacco, and meat make up most of the additional exports of foodstuffs.

A final item to note from Table IV is that under any of the alternatives the net changes in commodity flows would be in Canada's favour for each of the first four product divisions. It is the adverse net balance in the highly-manufactured-goods category that offsets the favourable results in the other four divisions.

Table V gives additional information on incremental trade flows by commodity group as estimated by the elasticities approach, including in this case specific consideration of agricultural goods[21] and fuels. While a full discussion of the impact of free trade on particular key industries must be deferred until the following chapter, several comments on the significance of this table are warranted. First, it makes clear that the exclusion of agricultural commodities from any free trade arrangement in which Canada participated would have a marked negative impact on the Canadian trade balance.

Second, given the extensive domestic agricultural-support policies and import restrictions practised by most countries (including those in the hypothetical free trade arrangements under review), we can say that the

[21]Defined to include not just the crude- and processed-foodstuffs and feed categories shown in Table IV, but also relevant portions of the crude- and semi-manufactured-materials categories. See footnote (*a*), Table V.

TABLE V

ESTIMATES OF STATIC EFFECTS OF VARIOUS FREE TRADE ALTERNATIVES ON 1966 CANADIAN
TRADE IN AGRICULTURAL COMMODITIES AND FUELS (million U.S. dollars)

| | Free trade partners | | | | |
|---|---|---|---|---|---|
| | USA (1) | USA and EFTA (2) | USA and J/A/NZ[a] (3) | J/A/NZ[a] (4) | USA, EFTA, EEC, J/A/NZ[a] (5) |
| *Agricultural goods[b]* | | | | | |
| Imports | 9 | 14 | 11 | 3 | 17 |
| Exports | 120 | 133 | 100 | 45 | 76 |
|    Net change in trade balance | +111 | +119 | +89 | +42 | +59 |
| *Fuels[c]* | | | | | |
| Imports | 10 | 10 | 10 | – | 10 |
| Exports | 7 | 7 | 7 | – | 7 |
|    Net change in trade balance | –3 | –3 | –3 | – | –3 |

[a]Japan, Australia, New Zealand.
[b]SITC Sections 0 and 1, Divisions 21, 22, 29, 41, 43, and groups 261–266.
[c]SITC Section 3.
Source: See text.

net trade gains to Canada suggested by this table are much below what they might be if all participating countries were to halt their non-tariff forms of protection. The EEC, Japan, and the United States are the chief offenders. Not only do their domestic policies cause imports from Canada to be lower than they otherwise would be, but, to the extent that they are subsidizing agricultural exports to third countries, they adversely affect Canadian exports to these countries too. Canada would have to compete with Australia and New Zealand in many of the relevant commodities—particularly meats—but even such competition would not prevent Canadian farmers from gaining substantially as a result of the freeing of production controls and trade restrictions in agricultural products. It is clear, therefore, that Canada should insist upon agricultural commodities being included in any free trade negotiations it undertakes.

Third, it is evident from Table V that fuels might as well have been excluded from the elasticity computations, for the increments obtained are negligible. We would simply remind the reader that Canadian exports of coal to Japan (and, to a lesser extent, other nations) and natural gas to the United States will likely grow rapidly without any changes in current trade arrangements. And without attempting any quantitative estimates at this juncture, we would add that if the United States opted for free trade in crude petroleum with Canada, while continuing to minimize reliance on non-continental sources, the expansion of Canadian fuel exports could be substantially more favourable than Table V suggests.

*Preferences for developing nations*[22]

A consideration we have omitted to this point concerns the impact that would be felt on the Canadian merchandise account from granting trade preferences to the developing nations concurrent with entry into a free trade arrangement. Precise answers are again impossible, but at least some clarification of the question can be attempted. In 1966 Canadian imports from the developing countries amounted to nearly U.S.$830 million. Of these imports, approximately two-thirds were duty-free, and, in addition, nearly one-sixth were crude materials and partially processed tropical products that would be quite insensitive to any further Canadian tariff reductions. If the tariffs on the remaining one-sixth of the imports, averaging about 12 percent,[23] were removed and an elasticity of −1.75 applied, the increase in Canadian imports from this source would be in the neighbourhood of U.S.$30 million, a relatively small amount.[24] This estimate does not allow, however, for the elimination of *de facto* import quotas (i.e., "voluntary" export restraints) on textiles and clothing from countries such as Hong Kong and Taiwan, which would undoubtedly affect the level of imports of such goods. Nor does it allow for the possibility that preferences to the developing countries by the advanced nations might see the initiation of "offshore production" by many international corporations. Where manufacturing entails relatively large amounts of unskilled labour, there can be huge cost advantages in establishing plants in these low-wage countries for export to Canada and other developed nations.[25]

This latter contingency goes beyond the static framework of the foregoing analysis. But it is worth pursuing the argument a little further at this juncture

[22]Material in this section was published earlier in B. W. Wilkinson, "Economic Cooperation in the Pacific: A Canadian Approach," *Journal of Common Market Studies*, 9, June 1971, pp. 320–1.

[23]G. L. Reuber, in "Canada's Economic Policies Toward the Less Developed Countries" (*Canadian Journal of Economics*, 1, Nov. 1968, p. 689), indicates that "the average tariff levied on dutiable imports from the LDC's on manufactures of special interest to the LDC's was 15.9 percent in 1966." Our number above reflects an adjustment for the Kennedy Round.

[24]Cf. Benjamin and Jean Higgins, *Canada's Trade Policy in the Second Development Decade*, Montreal, Canadian Economic Policy Committee, 1970, p. 45.

[25]A good review of the issues may be found in H. G. Johnson, "LDC Investment: The Road is Paved with Preferences," *Columbia Journal of World Business*, 3, Jan.-Feb., 1968, pp. 17–21.

so as to clarify the issues. Moreover, the discussion will provide a useful link with the subsequent section, where dynamic influences are examined somewhat more fully.

If international corporations were to initiate offshore production, the impact upon capital flows from the advanced nations to the developing countries and upon the imports of the advanced nations from the developing countries could be immense. If it were permitted to happen too quickly, it could have severe short-run effects upon the economies of the developed nations. The extent of these effects, however, will depend upon the strategies followed by the developing nations. The alternatives they might choose would include one or more of the following: increasing their imports in line with the increased capital inflows from, and exports to, the developed nations; revaluing their currencies; repaying their debts; and expanding their reserves.

If we assume their goal to be the most rapid economic development possible but that their ability to import has been inhibited by foreign-exchange shortages, then presumably they would choose the first alternative of using increased foreign-exchange earnings to expand imports. In this event, while the impact on gross flows of commodities would be enormous, the net change in the developed countries' merchandise trade balances (and, indeed, in their balances of payments and domestic employment) would not be too great. If the poorer nations chose to revalue their currencies—an unlikely possibility—there would again be no major adjustment problems. Debt repayment would generate no balance of payments difficulties for the developed nations as a whole, although expansionary domestic measures would likely be necessary to offset the negative impact of expanded imports on the merchandise trade balances of these nations. Finally, if they opted for some reserve increases, then those developed nations faring less well in the scramble for sales in the developing nations would still have the choice of devaluing their own currencies. The consumers in these nations would not necessarily be much worse off from a devaluation, because the resulting higher cost of imports would be offset by the lower costs of the cheap production abroad—to the extent, of course, that such goods were still imported.

In the long run, as the developing countries raised their standards of living, international unionism would probably see to it that a move towards equalization of wages occurred throughout the world in line with, or possibly in excess of, increasing productivity in the less developed lands. Some evidence of the growth of international unionism to counter the spread of the international corporation has already appeared.

The foregoing comments, of course, apply to all the developed nations granting the preferences, and not just to Canada alone. Canada, however, might not experience increases in gross flows of commodities or capital as massive as for some other nations. On the commodity side, Canada already imports a larger proportion of its domestic needs for many labour-intensive manufacturers than do a number of other major wealthy countries.[26] In the case of exports, Canada may not be as well prepared to benefit from new markets for investment and consumer products in the poorer nations. As for investment, the capital outflow from Canada to establish production facilities in the less developed nations would probably be relatively small, since this country is the base of few international corportions. And for this same reason any return flow of interest and dividend returns from investments abroad would also be limited.

*Synopsis*

In summary, Canadian participation in a free trade association with the United States, with the United States and EFTA, with the United States and Japan, Australia, and New Zealand, or with the last three countries alone would not be likely to cause a major balance of payments adjustment problem for Canada insofar as static trade effects are concerned. If the association were to include the EEC as well as the other developed countries just indicated, Canada could experience a significant deficit on merchandise account, running as high as one billion U.S. dollars, if domestic and foreign import-demand elasticities were very high. The deficit in this larger free trade group is much greater than under the other alternatives primarily because Canada would then be facing competition from all the major industrial nations and would not enjoy any preferences in the markets of any of these nations over other developed countries in the Western world. The deficits (or small surpluses) that occurred under the various free trade alternatives examined would be worse to the extent that preferences to the developing countries produced sizable increments in imports of labour-intensive manufactures that were not offset by shipments of other goods to these countries. On the other hand, the situation would be more favourable than indicated if exports of agricultural goods or fuels were expanded beyond what the elasticity results suggest. No quantification of these latter considerations has been attempted. Instead, in the remainder of the chapter, the numbers given in Table III are used as indicative of the magnitudes involved. The reader will be able to adjust our conclusions according to his own assessment of the strength of these other forces.

[26]To illustrate, the import of basic textiles per person in Canada is about double that for the United Kingdom, triple that for the United States, and five times that for the European Economic Community.

*Dynamic considerations*

ECONOMIES OF SCALE

The idea of greater economies of scale in production—and the dynamic effects that would arise therefrom—has been the most popular of the arguments made for Canadian involvement in some kind of free trade arrangement. The discussion has been confined largely to the impact on secondary manufacturing (equivalent to finished manufactures and chemicals in the trade classification used above) because many of the raw-material-producing and primary manufacturing industries have already attained sufficient scale economies to be able to export competitively. (In fact, exports often have been the means whereby these latter industries have achieved sufficient scale economies to make them internationally competitive.)

The proposition is that other nations' tariffs on Canadian secondary manufactures tend to limit the opportunities for exporting, and hence for achieving economies of scale in production, while the protection afforded by the Canadian tariff provides no incentive for firms in Canada to rationalize and obtain those scale economies attainable even within the confines of the Canadian market. The removal of foreign tariffs would provide a larger market for Canadian producers, and the removal of Canadian protection would offer the necessary stimulus to them to modernize and rationalize their production. Lower production costs and hence lower prices and a more internationally competitive secondary manufacturing industry would, it is suggested, be the outcome.

This reasoning suggests that, even for our fifth alternative, the *net* worsening of merchandise trade account, in turn owing to the deficit in trade of finished manufactures and chemicals, might well be less than the preceding static computations indicate. If the cost declines in Canadian secondary manufacturing were sufficient, it is conceivable that the worsened trade balance could be eliminated at the same time as the economy gained from greater productivity and efficiency.

We can illustrate the possible favourable impact of cost reductions upon the Canadian trade balance with a simple model. First, assume the absence of any changes in non-merchandise trade, capital flows, exchange rates, or foreign prices.[27] Assume, as well, that Canadian price reductions match

[27]This assumes that our trading partners have already achieved most of the possible economies of scale in production and therefore could not expect significant price decreases from this source in any new free trade arrangement. For the United States, Japan, the EEC, and the EFTA countries, each of which already has tariff-free access to markets of 85 million or more, this would seem a reasonably accurate supposition. It would also seem probable that the lowering of these countries' own tariffs would not greatly reduce their domestic production costs or, alternatively, that any reductions

cost improvements emanating from the attainment of scale economies and occur at the same time as the tariff removal.[28] Finally, assume that for Canadian exports the effects of both the price decrease and the tariff elimination abroad apply to the initial value of exports adjusted downward for the price decrease and that these two effects are additive. Then, it can be shown that the price (and related cost) declines necessary to avoid an adverse change in the Canadian merchandise trade balance in the event of free trade with the other major developed nations (alternative 5) are in the 3.7 to 4.6 percent range, depending upon whether the high, medium, or low import elasticities are presumed to apply.[29]

Other factors could make the necessary total cost decline greater or less than these numbers suggest. On the one hand, if foreign producers chose to reduce their prices somewhat in the face of increased Canadian competition, then the Canadian cost reductions would have to be that much greater. In the extreme, if foreigners matched Canadian producers' price declines, then a devaluation of the Canadian dollar might be required. This possibility is explored a little more in the following section.

On the other hand, our calculations assumed that production costs in other than secondary manufacturing remained constant. If allowance were made for lowered costs and therefore lowered prices in these other sectors as well, owing to lowered prices of inputs supplied by Canadian secondary manu-

---

that would occur would no more than offset the cost-push effects of any improvement in their balances of trade owing to free trade. The position would be much less likely to hold for Australia and New Zealand, which would presumably hope to enjoy the same economies in production that Canada desires. However, because of the minor role of these nations in Canadian trade, the inappropriateness of our assumption for them will not materially alter our conclusions.

[28]Implicit in this assumption is the further one that actually there will be some transition period in which tariffs are removed and industry rationalizes. Many industries may be able to rationalize quite quickly because they will not need to build new plants but only reduce the number of lines produced in their existing plants.

[29]The model used is:

$$Y = \sum_j [(t_{1j}/(1 + t_{1j})) - X]M_{1j}E_1 + \sum_i \{XM_{i1} - [(t_{i1}/(1 + t_{i1})) + X][M_{i1}(1 - X)E_i]\}$$

where: $t_{ij}$ = the tariff rate of country $i$ on imports from country $j$; $M_{ij}$ = the value of imports by country $i$ from country $j$; $E_i$ = country $i$ price elasticity of demand for imports; $X$ = the percentage price decline in Canadian exports and import-competing products. Country 1 is Canada, and the remaining countries are Canada's free trade partners. $Y$ = the total improvement in the trade balance for the first four commodity divisions—that is, for commodities other than highly manufactured goods. The price decline, $X$, must be sufficient to reduce the net adverse change in the trade balance in finished manufactures and chemicals to the value of this improvement. The first integration represents the net increase in the value of imports from free trade when there is a domestic price decrease of $X$ percent. The second integration represents the net expansion of Canadian exports resulting from the removal of foreign tariffs and the reduction of Canadian prices.

facturing,[30] then the surplus on merchandise trade in these sectors resulting from free trade would be greater than indicated. Consequently, the price decline in secondary manufacturing necessary to eliminate the unfavourable change in the merchandise account would be reduced from the 3.7 to 4.6 percent range estimated earlier.

In any event, the magnitude of the cost improvements for Canadian secondary manufactures appears attainable. The Wonnacotts[31] have shown that if similar scales of production were achieved in Canada and the United States, Canada would enjoy lower production costs in many industries, primarily because of lower Canadian wage rates. For example, if productivity in the two countries were equal, lower Canadian wage rates might permit Canadian prices to decrease by as much as 6 to 9 percent.[32]

Before going on to other dynamic considerations that would affect the manufacturing sector, it should be stressed that once industrial structure has been rationalized so as to supply the Canadian market more efficiently in the absence of protection, some producers are bound to be able to sell a larger share of their output in Canada. The number of such suppliers depends on the scale required for efficient supply and on the size of the Canadian market for the particular product. For many there will be a better reason for locating within the Canadian market than ever before because protective devices no longer will be contributing to excessive numbers of undersized producers and the more appropriate scale of successful suppliers will enable them to compete effectively at home and in the most readily accessible external markets, notably in the northern United States. Many of the dynamic effects to be discussed are closely related to this changed structure.

OTHER DYNAMIC CONSIDERATIONS

Although a detailed discussion of the adjustment process must await a later chapter, brief mention needs to be made, before concluding this one, of additional factors influencing the outcome of trade flows under free trade conditions, particularly as they relate to highly manufactured goods, where the bulk of the adjustments will occur. New technology, scale economies in

---

[30]Ignored is the possibility that lower prices may also occur owing to tariff elimination on imports of materials and equipment. Such static effects presumably should be subsumed in the import-demand elasticities used initially.

[31]Ronald J. Wonnacott and Paul Wonnacott, *Free Trade Between Canada and the United States*, Cambridge, Harvard University Press, 1967.

This statement is based on the assumptions that Canadian money wages in manufacturing are approximately 25 to 30 percent lower than those prevailing in the United States and that labour costs amount to between 25 to 30 percent of total production costs.

[32]Saburo Okita, in "Japan: A Resource Importing Nation" (*Chuo Koron*, Dec. 1967), estimated that GNP *per acre* in Japan is three times that for the United States.

marketing, foreign (particularly American) ownership of Canadian manufacturing, and management initiative and resourcefulness are all of significance.

Let us consider these issues initially in relation to a Canada-U.S. free
trade association and from the viewpoint of the American parent firms which
own much of Canadian manufacturing. With the possibility of greatly improved scale economies in production and the lower prevailing Canadian
wage rates, there would be an attraction for these firms to locate production
in Canada—at least in the Ottawa Valley and the Niagara Peninsula segments of Canada—to serve the American market. If this occurred, the
expansion of exports relative to imports could be substantially greater than
the static results suggest.

Whether such a trend occurred would depend upon management's assessment of these factors and other countervailing forces in the situation.
Research and development, a vital source of trade advantage, has largely
been undertaken to date by American firms on their home ground, close to
senior management and to a large industrial and market area where an
abundance of specialized technical services exist. Initial production will
probably continue to take place where the research is centred. Unless Canadian governments or management could convince the foreign corporations
that there are also cost advantages to doing more of their research in Canada,
this country would be unlikely to see much additional production based on
the very newest technology. Rather, Canada could at best expect to get the
production at a later stage in the product cycle, when low wages become
more important. If, however, under a Canada-U.S. agreement, tariff preferences were concurrently offered to the developing countries, they would
tend to get this low-wage production instead of Canada.

Furthermore, rationalization of Canadian industry will undoubtedly necessitate mergers of one form or another. Canadian laws will have to ensure
that, where such mergers are in Canadian interests, they will proceed without
regard to any objections that the United States may have because of its own
anti-combines regulations. If Canada is not free to proceed as its own advantage demands, its rationalization policies will be hamstrung. This would be
an unacceptable outcome.

Other issues must also be faced squarely. American investors might be
deterred by fear of the ultimate collapse of the free trade arrangement with
Canada or by apprehension lest international unions force up Canadian
wages soon after production locates in Canada so as to yield little net advantage from such location. There are, moreover, marketing cost advantages
to being located near the centres where purchases are the greatest. Quick
delivery becomes possible, follow-up consulting and repair services may be

rendered more easily, and buyer preferences may be more readily sampled and catered to. If these factors discouraging Canadian production were to dominate executive thinking, the merchandise balance from trade liberalization would be less favourable than indicated earlier.

Where Canadian-owned firms are involved and the research is undertaken domestically, new products would most likely be produced in Canada initially. But beyond this early stage, the arguments favouring some shift of production abroad would again be valid, and the net effect of these dynamic forces could go either against, or in favour of, Canada.

Were the free trade arrangement to be with other nations as well as the United States (i.e., alternatives 2, 3, or 5), much the same considerations apply. The main difference is that the probability of Canada's receiving any low-wage production would be reduced even more. Canada's capability to produce and export sophisticated manufactures would depend to a still greater extent upon Canadian management initiatives in undertaking research and development to produce differentiated competitive commodities and in establishing suitable marketing channels abroad. Where firms were foreign-owned, success would also depend, at least in part, upon the initiatives of the Canadian side of management in convincing the parent firm to permit production, and hopefully research, in the Canadian subsidiary for the international market.

Finally, consider the fourth alternative of free trade—including Japan, Australia, and New Zealand, but excluding the United States. Once again Canada would not be the centre for low-wage production. As the Japanese permit more firms to enter, either with 100 percent foreign ownership or with up to 50 percent foreign ownership, depending on the industry, growing numbers of Canadian or other non-Japanese firms may locate in Japan to take advantage of lower wage rates there for exports back to Canada. Not only would there probably occur a tremendous diversion of Canadian imports of sophisticated products from the United States to Japan (beyond what our static estimates suggest), but there could easily be a net expansion of *total* imports and some diversion of foreign capital flows from Canada to Japan. Offsetting these changes in part, Canadian exports of agricultural products could be increased greatly as Japan disbanded its elaborate system of high internal markups on imported commodities, domestic subsidies, and other protective measures. (Canada would, of course, have to compete with Australia and New Zealand in selling agricultural goods to Japan.) Concomitantly, Canadian exports to Japan of minerals and coal should continue to expand, not so much from the reduction of Japanese protectionism, but from the continued growth of the Japanese economy. Hopefully, as Japanese tariffs are lowered on semi-processed materials and products at more advanced stages of production, Canada should be able to make more of its sales in these products, rather than simply shipping minerals in their crudest form as is now the case. Additional processing in Canada would be in accord with the wealth of energy resources, mineral resources, and water existing in Canada. It would also be consistent with the Japanese shortage of all these resources and the extremely high density of economic activity already existing in Japan.[33]

EXCHANGE-RATE ADJUSTMENTS

To conclude this discussion, we can indicate the approximate magnitude of the exchange-rate adjustment that might be necessary should an adverse change in the merchandise trade balance take place. For simplicity, and because it is consistent with our goal of presenting the most unfavourable situation for Canada, we shall assume away the possibility that the attainment of production scale economies will lead to lower prices for Canadian exports and import-competing goods. At the same time, however, we shall assume initially that Canadian prices of exports and import-competing goods reflect the full amount of any devaluation. Foreign prices and exchange rates and, of course, domestic and foreign incomes are assumed to remain unchanged. Deviations in capital flows are ignored, and the medium price elasticities of demand for imports are presumed the relevant ones.[34] For consistency with our earlier analysis, the 1966 trade flows were used.

Given these assumptions, it can be shown that a one percent drop in the value of the Canadian dollar would produce an improvement in the Canadian merchandise trade balance of between U.S.$175 million and U.S.$200 million.[35] (If the low or high elasticities were the relevant ones, the improvement would be one-half or double this amount, respectively.) In other words, the size of the devaluation necessary to offset the worsening of the trade balance when the static results are those of a Canada-U.S.-EFTA-EEC-Japan-Australia-New Zealand agreement would be in the order of 2.5 percent—a modest adjustment indeed.

Devaluation would raise Canadian production costs directly by increasing the prices of imported materials and equipment. It would augment production costs indirectly, too, by inflating consumer-goods' prices. Such inflation,

[33]For additional comment on a Canadian trade association with Japan, see B. W. Wilkinson, "Economic Co-operation in the Pacific: A Canadian Approach" (a paper presented to the Pacific Conference, Vina del Mar, Chile, Sept. 27–Oct. 3, 1970). The above discussion draws in part on that paper.
[34]We ignore the fact that exchange-rate elasticities are frequently observed to be less than tariff elasticities.
[35]The reasoning used in deriving this estimate is similar to that used in the formulation of the model in footnote 29, p. 66.

in turn, would be likely to cause money-wage increases as workers tried to maintain the purchasing power of their incomes. Hence, a one percent devaluation might enhance the country's international competitiveness by less than one percent. If competitiveness were improved by only 0.65 percent,[36] then at most a 3.9 percent devaluation would be necessary to avoid any adverse change in trade balance.[37] If there were any resulting net improvements in the non-merchandise trade account, the required devaluation would be less than this. The sensitivity of this latter account to exchange-rate changes is not likely to be great, however, and in keeping with our intention of taking a conservative position on the beneficial effects of adjustments to free trade, we shall not adjust the above estimate to reflect any improvement in it. Changes in capital flows would similarly alter the results.

In any event, what should be clear and what should be emphasized is that even in the extreme situation of free trade among all the major developed countries—the situation that would produce the most unfavourable impact, among the alternatives examined, upon the Canadian balance of merchandise trade—the size of the net adjustment in domestic production costs or exchange rates is relatively small in aggregate. The adjustment for particular sectors, of course, might be substantial and require government assistance on a major scale to ease the burden on particular firms or segments of the labour force. Adverse capital flows could also make the adjustment problem greater. So could the failure of international corporations to follow policies consistent with the objectives of the Canadian government and with Canadian interests. But these are matters for subsequent chapters.

*Recent developments*

Important changes have taken place in the world since 1966, the year used in estimating the trade-flow changes in this chapter. Although in our computations allowance was made for the Kennedy Round tariff changes and for

---

[36]R. N. Cooper estimates for Britain that "a 1 percent devaluation would improve Britain's relative price competitiveness by 0.70 percent" ("The Balance of Payments," *Britain's Economic Prospects,* ed. Richard E. Caves and Associates, Washington, Brookings Institution, 1968, pp. 191–2). Detailed information such as he used for Britain in arriving at this figure was not available for Canada at the time of writing. But if no other countries but Canada were to devalue (whereas with Britain, at least some other nations generally follow its lead) and with the import content of exports and domestic final demand apparently about the same for Canada as for Britain, then a 0.65 percent improvement in competitiveness from a one percent devaluation if anything errs on the low side.

[37]Again notice we have assumed that any beneficial effect of lowered tariffs on the costs of imported materials and capital equipment has been reflected already in the elasticity estimates employed. If this were not so, then our original estimate of 2.5 percent would be the more appropriate one.

the exchange-rate changes up to 1969, we did not allow for the growth and altered structure of Canadian trade since 1966, the major changes in exchange rates that have taken place in the early 1970s, or British entry into the Common Market.

Limitations of time and resources did not permit the preparation and analysis of new data to reflect these developments in detail prior to the publication of this summary volume. But some rough indications of their effects are possible.

Consider, first, alterations in Canadian trade. Between 1966 and 1971, Canadian exports and imports rose 72 percent and 54 percent, respectively. If automotive equipment is excluded, the increments are reduced substantially—to 44 percent and 36 percent, respectively. Over the same period, the total merchandise trade surplus increased from $225 million to $2,200 million. Of this improvement, $820 million is attributable to the auto pact, leaving $1,200 million to be explained by other forces—such as the recession of the Canadian economy, with its accompanying depressing effect upon imports.

If the analysis had been based entirely upon 1971 trade, then, expectations are that the greater value of trade would tend to raise the estimates of the adverse effects of free trade on the merchandise-account balance. The strengthened merchandise surplus, however, would work in the opposite direction. Rough computations indicate that the net effect of these opposing influences under free trade with other developed countries (alternative 5) would be to expand the adverse trade change by about $150 million to around $625 million. The size of the price reduction that would have to be achieved from scale economies to eliminate this deficit—or, alternately, the devaluation required—would not be changed significantly from the estimates presented earlier in the chapter.

A number of qualifications to these conclusions are necessary. The full adverse impact of the appreciation of the Canadian dollar by nearly 8 percent in the months following its unpegging on June 1, 1970, was not fully reflected in 1971. And as the Canadian economy struggles back to something approximating full employment, the trade surplus registered in 1971 will be reduced further. The entry of Britain into the Common Market also will handicap some Canadian exports to that country. Finally, the United States has passed the DISC (Domestic International Sales Corporation) legislation, which permits almost indefinite deferral of half the normal corporate income tax on net revenues earned from exports and confers a significant competitive advantage upon American-based production.[38]

38The DISC law on average will provide manufacturers in the United States a 2–4 percent price advantage over Canadian producers compared to what they had prior

Offsetting in part these unfavourable forces are two influences. First, the gradual recovery of the American economy will expand the demand for a wide range of Canadian products, both in the United States and in other economies depending partly upon the U.S. economy for their own prosperity. Second, with regard to nations other than the United States, the realignment of exchange rates in December, 1971, will counter the dampening influence on the Canadian merchandise trade surplus of the 1970 appreciation of the Canadian dollar.[39]

The sum total of these positive and negative influences probably will be adverse. With a flexible Canadian rate, adjustment can, of course, occur through a decline in the value of the Canadian dollar—unless offset by capital inflows. This adjustment issue is examined more fully in the next chapter. For now it is sufficient to observe that, in spite of any adjustment advantage that a flexible exchange rate may confer, the present situation strongly supports the argument that rationalization of Canadian manufacturing is a matter of increasing urgency.

## Appendix A

A. JUSTIFICATION FOR THE ASSUMPTION OF PERFECTLY ELASTIC SUPPLIES
   BY EXPORTING COUNTRIES IN ESTIMATES OF TRADE-CREATION EFFECTS

For the United States, exports in general comprise only a small proportion of total output. Increased supplies should be forthcoming without necessitating significant price increases.

For Japan, exports comprise about 12 to 15 percent of gross domestic product, and Japan most likely would enjoy a sizable net improvement in its trade balance under free trade arrangements with other developed nations.[1] Hence, the possibility of less than perfectly elastic export-supply elasticities is not so easily discounted. Yet, provided agricultural products were an integral part of any free trade arrangement, the consequent release of labour from the inefficient agricultural sector (still comprising 20 percent of the Japanese labour force) and lower food prices from cheaper imports would help to ease any upward pressure on labour costs and therefore on

---

to this legislation. Other tax concessions provided in the U.S. Revenue Act of 1971 would give producers another 2 percent advantage. See B. W. Wilkinson, "Recent American Tax Concessions to Industry and Canadian Economic Policy," *Canadian Tax Journal*, Jan.–Feb., 1972, pp. 1–14.

[39]The French franc and the British pound were both revalued by 8.6 percent, while the German mark and Japanese yen were revalued 13.6 percent and 16.9 percent, respectively.

[1]See B. W. Wilkinson, "A Re-estimation of the Effects of the Formation of a Pacific Area Trade Agreement," *Pacific Trade and Development*, 2, pp. 53–101.

prices of manufactures. Improved efficiency of the service sector, at present employing over 40 percent of the Japanese work force, would provide another source of labour to meet the needs of an expanding manufacturing sector without major price increases. Consequently, we retain the assumption of perfectly elastic export supplies for Japan.

For the United Kingdom, another major Canadian supplier, exports equal about 15 percent of gross domestic product. Even here, however, although the British balance of trade is likely to improve from any free trade arrangement that included Canada and Britain,[2] there would seem to be room for more efficient use of labour resources in that economy.[3] Free trade beyond the present EFTA boundaries might well be the stimulus necessary for such a reallocation of resources to occur. It does not seem unreasonable to preserve the perfectly elastic export-supply assumption for the United Kingdom. The same assumption may be less appropriate for a number of the remaining industrial countries in Europe. But because of the very small proportion of Canadian imports accounted for by these nations, the total impact on the Canadian trade balance would differ little one way or the other whether or not perfectly elastic export supplies are assumed. For simplicity, then, the assumption of perfect elasticity is maintained for these countries.

Australia, New Zealand, and Canada hope to achieve economies of scale and greater productivity through production for export. Also, the contribution to lower production costs through the removal of tariffs on imports of materials and equipment is likely to be greater for these countries than for those mentioned above. Both forces would give a downward bias to their prices. With regard to the potential for lower production costs from scale economies, witness the enormous increase in Canadian exports of automobiles and parts[4] to the United States in recent years, accompanied by a *drop* in the average price of Canadian-built cars. Only if bottlenecks arose, or if a general factor-price rise occurred because of full employment and inflation generated by much improved trade balances, would the tendency be for export prices to increase noticeably. But general demand pressures would be unlikely for any of these countries because free trade would result in a worsening, or at best a very small improvement, in their trade balances.[5] In addition, for Canada labour-force growth rates have been high, and are

[2]Maxwell Stamp Associates, *The Free Trade Area Option: Opportunity for Britain*, London, The Atlantic Trade Study, 1967, pp. 45–56.
[3]See Lloyd Ulman, "Collective Bargaining and Industrial Efficiency," *Britain's Economic Prospects*, ed. Richard E. Caves and Associates, Washington, Brookings Institution, 1968, pp. 324–80.
[4]As discussed in Chap. 2.
[5]For Canada see the results in the text, and for Australia and New Zealand see B. W. Wilkinson, "A Re-estimation ..."

anticipated to continue high, in relation to both recent and anticipated growth rates in other industrialized countries. Consequently, new labour-force entrants may be expected to be adequate to satisfy any increased demands for labour emanating from greater exports in specific sectors.

In general, then, the assumption of perfectly elastic export supplies would seem to be an acceptable simplification.

B. DETAILS ON TARIFFS AND THE COMPUTATIONS OF TRADE CREATION
AND TRADE DIVERSION

(a) GATT tariff rates and, where appropriate, British preferential rates for the years both prior to and after the Kennedy Round were estimated for each group by unweighted averaging of the individual applicable rates.[6] Two types of exceptions were made in this procedure. First, in those instances where rates prevailing between Australia, New Zealand, and Canada as a result of bilateral agreements between these nations differed from their British preferential rates, the British preferential rates were used for simplicity. The second exception occurred with regard to the EFTA nations other than Britain. Because of the very small proportion of Canadian exports to these countries (particularly in the more sensitive commodity categories) and the high proportion of specific rates that would have had to be converted to *ad valorem* rates (all Swiss and Portuguese rates are specific), only rough estimates were made of their tariffs. Averages from existing sources[7] were used and adjusted in a broad way for the Dillon and Kennedy Rounds of tariff reductions.

Rates for Australia, Canada, and the United States were adjusted downward 10 percent to allow for the fact that imports are recorded f.o.b. rather than c.i.f. in these countries.[8] U.S. duties on benzenoid chemicals were doubled to reflect the impact of the American Selling Price method of valuation on imports of these goods.[9] Shipments of motor vehicles and parts between Canada and the United States were all assumed to have duty-free pre-Kennedy Round rates, even though replacement parts are not included in the Canada-U.S. automotive agreement. Nominal, not effective, tariffs were

[6]The *International Customs Journal* and GATT reports on the Kennedy Round were used.
[7]Political and Economic Planning, *Atlantic Tariffs and Trade*, London, George Allen and Unwin, 1962, and broad adjustments for the Dillon and Kennedy Rounds of tariff negotiation.
[8]See Frances K. Topping, *Comparative Tariffs and Trade*, Committee for Economic Development, 1963, vol. 1, p. XIII.
[9]See Political and Economic Planning, *Atlantic Tariffs and Trade*, London, George Allen and Unwin, 1962, p. xvi; also H. G. Grubel and H. G. Johnson, "Nominal Tariff Rates and United States Valuation Practices: Two Case Studies," *Review of Economics and Statistics*, 49, May 1967, pp. 138–42.

used throughout the computations, an appropriate arrangement when the direct method of applying elasticities of demand for imports to the tariff changes is employed—as was done in this study. Balassa, for example, found that the differences in trade changes resulting from using the above method— as opposed to the indirect approach involving domestic elasticities of demand for importables and supply of value added of importables, as well as both nominal and effective rates—were generally small and never in excess of 10 percent.[10] Moreover, the assumptions required in arriving at effective rates make it extremely questionable whether they can be used with any precision or confidence in estimating effects of tariff reductions.

The Common External Tariff of the EEC was not fully implemented until July 1, 1968, and in 1966 the tariffs of the participating nations had been moved only 60 percent of the way to the CET level. But with the rates of some countries still above the CET in 1966 and some below it, use of the CET seemed a good compromise. The removal of tariffs among the individual EEC members was not finished in 1966 either, being only 80 percent complete on industrial products by the first of that year and only 60–65 percent complete for agricultural products. Similarly, among the EFTA countries in 1966, 20 percent of each nation's tariff to outsiders still remained in trade among them. These complications were ignored in our estimates. Initial rough computations indicated that to allow for them would have lowered Canadian exports by no more than a very few millions of dollars.

(b) Anyone who compares the above results under the third of our alternatives—a free trade arrangement among Canada, the United States, Japan, Australia, and New Zealand—with those presented in an earlier paper[11] will note a discrepancy between them. The extra trade-creation effects and the trade-diversion effects under the medium elasticity assumptions in the latter paper (Appendix Table A-7 less Appendix Table A-5), which are the same elasticity assumptions used here, are greater than those indicated above for Canada. There are two reasons for this. First, in the earlier paper, the rest of the world was assumed to be not only the developed countries of the Western world, as assumed in the present study, but all nations. For the reasons given on page 12 of the text, it was thought to be more appropriate to include only the developed countries when making these computations. Second, the method used for allocating the extra trade-creation effects among nations in the present study was somewhat different from that employed in the earlier work and gives more conservative results. This is in accord with our desire to give the least favourable position for

[10]*Trade Liberalization Among Industrial Countries: Objectives and Alternatives,* New York, McGraw-Hill, 1967, p. 77.
[11]B. W. Wilkinson, "A Re-estimation ..."

Canadian trade that might emanate from participation in any free trade arrangement.

(c) Commodity divisions, groups, and subgroups from the Standard International Trade Classification[12] distinguished in this study:

(1) Crude foodstuffs and feed:

00, 04, 05, 06, 07, 08, 09, 121.

(2) Processed foodstuffs and feed:

01, 02, 03, 111, 112, 122.

(3) Crude materials:

21, 22, 231.1, 231.3, 231.4, 241, 244, 26, 27, 28, 29, 32, 331, 34, 35, 41.

(4) Semi-manufactures (non-food):

242, 243, 251, 42, 43, 61, 62, 631–633, 661–664, 671, 672, 681–689.

(5) Finished-manufactures and chemicals:

231.2, 332, 51–59, 641.1, 641.2–641.9, 642, 651–657, 665–667, 673–679, 691–698, 711–899.

[12]For details, see Statistical Office of the United Nations, *Statistical Papers,* Series M, No. 34, New York, 1961.

# 5. Free Trade and the Structure of the Canadian Economy

During the past five or six years, much more work has been done in Canada than ever before to assess the specific implications of industrial free trade for the Canadian economy. A good many of these studies were undertaken and prepared under the Atlantic Economic Studies Program of the Private Planning Association of Canada. But several others were prepared earlier or concurrently under various auspices.

Among the latter, probably the earliest of the notable works on industrial structure was a study published in 1957 for the Royal Commission on Canada's Economic Prospects (Gordon Commission), *Canadian Secondary Manufacturing Industry*, by D. H. Fullerton and H. A. Hampson. These authors illuminated some of the structural deficiencies in various Canadian manufacturing industries. In 1964, H. E. English's *Industrial Structure in Canada's International Competitive Position*[1] probed more deeply into selected industries, examining the effects of trade barriers on the structure and conduct of Canada's chemicals, industrial-machinery, and consumer-durables sectors. A similar type of analysis covering a broader range of industries was published in 1967 by H. C. Eastman and the late Stefan Stykolt, *The Tariff and Competition in Canada*.[2] Industries analyzed in the Eastman-Stykolt report included fruit and vegetable canning, cement, container board, shipping containers, synthetic detergents, major electrical appliances, newsprint, meat packing, petroleum refining, steel, and rubber tires. An equally wide range, but somewhat different assortment, of industries was similarly analyzed in a staff study for the Economic Council of Canada, *Scale and Specialization in Canadian Manufacturing*, prepared by D. J. Daly, B. A. Keys, and E. J. Spence and published in 1968. Although these various studies had somewhat different specific purposes, they all had the effect of drawing attention to some of the implications of trade liberalization.

---

[1]H. E. English, *Industrial Structure in Canada's International Competitive Position*, Montreal, Canadian Trade Committee, 1964.
[2]H. C. Eastman and Stefan Stykolt, *The Tariff and Competition in Canada*, Toronto, Macmillan, 1967.

One of the most comprehensive studies, as well as the first that specifically addressed itself to the free-trade-impact question, was the 1967 book by Ronald and Paul Wonnacott, *Free Trade Between the United States and Canada: The Potential Economic Effects.*[3] A shorter version of this book, and one which focused the impact analysis more on Canada, was published by the Canadian-American Committee in 1968 under the title *U.S.-Canadian Free Trade: The Potential Impact on the Canadian Economy.* The Wonnacotts ranked the economic regions of Canada and the United States (using five Canadian and thirteen U.S. regions) with respect to two kinds of influence relevant to the location of each of the many manufacturing industries they covered. The first was that of factor prices, notably wage rates and resource, transportation, and capital costs. The second was a set of "proximity" factors, such as closeness to markets, to manufactured supplies, and to industry agglomerations that give rise to supply and other external economies. In addition, the Wonnacotts examined certain product groups (such as automobiles, furniture, and wrapping paper) in particular detail.

The factor-price part of the Wonnacotts' findings has naturally been affected by the pasage of time and by changes in relative costs between regions and industries—notably the narrowing of some wage-rate differentials between U.S. and Canadian regions. But even that part of their analysis continues to provide a helpful base from which to take into account some of the changes that have since occurred in factor costs; and, in fact, later studies have progressively developed the factor-cost data for some industries.

The Wonnacotts' "proximity" approach to the ranking of regions appears to have maintained its full value with the pasage of time. On the basis of proximity factors, they gave the highest regional ranking to the "industrial heartland" running roughly from Chicago to Boston to Baltimore. However, as they pointed out, the real question, from the Canadian standpoint, is not, Which North American region is the "best" location for each kind of manufacturing? Rather, the basic issue is, Since each broad class of manufacturing is carried on in several U.S. regions in addition to the "best'" location for each class, does not Canada also contain regions that would be able to support certain restructured and more-specialized manufacturing industries under free trade? In their analysis, the Wonnacotts pointed out that (1) the manufacturing belt in southern Ontario and Quebec lies partly within, and in any event very close to, the U.S. heartland triangle—closer to it, in fact, than any non-heartland U.S. region, with the possible exception of New England; (2) with reference to the four proximity factors taken together,

[3]Ronald J. Wonnacott and Paul Wonnacott, *Free Trade Between the United States and Canada: The Potential Economic Effects*, Cambridge, Massachusetts, Harvard University Press, 1967.

Ontario and Quebec rank higher than any of the non-heartland regions; (3) in the heartland region, two influences operate in opposite directions: while producers generally have some desire to locate close to major markets and agglomerations of supply, at the same time they generally have some desire to avoid areas already heavily serviced by competitors and also giving rise to some diseconomies of congestion, the latter consideration tending to favour the better of the non-heartland regions; (4) meanwhile, if Ontario and Quebec can retain *any* of their wage-rate advantage, so much the better for their attractiveness as industrial locations. For Canadian regions other than southern Ontario and Quebec, the relevant question for the Wonnacotts was whether these other regions, being presently disadvantaged by protection, would find their situation improved by free trade. One obvious and major improvement, they noted, was that these other regions would, under free trade, pay lower prices than at present for manufactured goods produced in both central Canada and the United States.

The Atlantic Economic Studies Program of the Private Planning Association tried to focus more directly and in greater depth on selected industries and regions of Canada in examining the implications of trade liberalization. In addition to these regional and industrial studies, several of a more general nature were undertaken relating to such questions as transitional or adjustment mechanisms, capital-flow considerations, transportation factors, and the degrees of need or lack of need to harmonize other national economic policies in the event of increasingly freer trade. The industries selected for impact analysis included agriculture, various mining and petroleum products, primary iron and steel, pulp and paper products, and furniture. The region studied was British Columbia.

Several principles of selection governed the choice of industries: (1) the desirability of examining a range of industrial situations, including some that have traditionally engaged in export activity and others that have relied on a domestic market (usually a protected domestic market); (2) the desirability of looking at industries covering a range of products and at least some product differentiation (for example, agriculture, paper, and furniture), a mixture of domestic and foreign ownership (mining and petroleum, primary iron and steel, and paper), and variety in other dimensions; (3) the desirability of avoiding duplication of studies on industries that had received, or were known to be receiving, the attention of others (one example was the automotive industry, a study of which was being undertaken by Carl E. Beigie for the Canadian-American Committee and was published in 1970; some of the findings of this study will be included in our discussion).

It is important to be aware of what sorts of things the study of individual industries can and cannot tell us about the impact of freer trade. Since international trade theory assures us that there are invariably some lines of activity in which any country has a comparative advantage no matter how inferior its resource endowments, one scarcely needs empirical assurance that benefits from trade are available. However, since the locus of comparative advantages for any country cannot be determined by a limited range of particular studies, one cannot really predict the implications of free trade either for an individual industry or for an economy as a whole by this means. Essentially, the study of a group of industries serves a number of more limited purposes:

1. It offers an opportunity to identify the relative advantages of particular lines of products within the range produced by an industry. Thus, one can identify the most probable lines of specialization, given the assumption that the industry will survive in the face of international competition.

2. It offers a realistic context for examining the effects of discarding simplifying assumptions such as zero transport costs, constant costs, pure competition, and unduly limited patterns of size and space distribution of markets.

3. It affords an opportunity for more specific identification of factors of production, their qualitative differences, and the extent to which technology may compensate for relative scarcities. The literature on international trade has been overburdened with misleadingly simplified factor analyses.

If examination of the impact of trade liberalization upon specific industries can cast any light on the foregoing questions, this in turn can result in an increase in the relevance of much public discussion of the issues. We can perhaps avoid the kind of casual empiricism that identifies the competitive problems or adjustment difficulties of a particular industry and then generalizes about all manufacturing.

A good example of such casual empiricism has been the case of agricultural machinery. Since a wide range of these products has been freely traded since 1944, an opportunity has been afforded to observe some of the effects of trade liberalization on a manufacturing industry. Politicians and even some members of the professional establishment have cited the experience of this industry as constituting a warning against free trade for Canada. Much of the problem has arisen out of a superficial analysis of the historical record. For example, it has sometimes been said that, because of free trade, Canada failed to develop tractor production in the postwar period. This interpretation neglects the fact that, except for the highly protected conditions prevailing during World War II and the immediate postwar years, Canada has never been a significant manufacturer of farm tractors. Another superficial view has been to cite the slow growth of Canadian agricultural-machinery production during the later 1950s as evidence that it was free trade that prevented Canada from keeping up with U.S. production. This naive interpretation of the record neglects certain features of the corporate history of the industry during these years, but, more important, neglects the overvaluation of the Canadian dollar—a circumstance that was bound to affect especially adversely one of the few Canadian manufacturing industries that was highly export-oriented in those years. Following the correction of that unwarranted overvaluation in the early 1960s, the agricultural-machinery industry has grown in relation to the U.S. industry to the point that its output has been restored to approximately the same relative position it enjoyed in the early 1950s. A longer-term statistical comparison—the late 1920s with the mid-1960s—shows a similar stability in the overall Canada-U.S. relative shares in output and trade. However, trade flows in the postwar years were concentrated in the north-south direction, whereas in earlier years overseas countries had been more important, especially as a market for Canadian exports.

The maintenance of Canada's relative share of overall production in this industry would seem to warrant a rather favourable inference concerning the effects of free trade on certain other Canadian industries, since important locational considerations favour Canada less in the agricultural-machinery industry than in the production of other durables, including other types of machinery as well as consumer durables. For agricultural machinery, the bulk of the North American market lies well to the west of the manufacturing heart of Canada in southern Ontario and much closer to the U.S. manufacturing cities around the southern end of Lake Michigan, while for other durables both the Canadian market and the general North American market usually favour locations in the lower Lakes regions. It should be added, in this connection, that the firms which produce agricultural machinery produce also, in some cases, non-agricultural machinery, but are deterred from supplying the North American market from their Canadian plants because of the absence of free trade for these product lines.

The variety of circumstances affecting the implications of trade liberalization can be further identified from other industry studies, several of which were undertaken under the AESP program. David Quirin, in his study of non-ferrous metal and petroleum products, was unable to develop adequate data for a few of the sectors that would have made the study comprehensive, representative, and complete, and so the study will not be published. However, the completed sections, which cover a majority of representative sectors, are worth reporting upon in the present context.

The portions on non-ferrous metals confirm our expectation that free trade could extend opportunities for Canadian processing and fabricating, as well as production, of non-ferrous metals. In the past, it has been most profitable to concentrate on primary production. Probably the best opportunity to pre-empt a larger share of North American and world markets for processed metals occurred in the 1950s, before other countries developed their own processing capacities in the years following the shortages of World War II and in the reconstruction era that followed. The failure of Canadian governments, and also perhaps of firms in the industry themselves, to try to capture larger external markets during that period has left these producers with a more formidable task now that foreign governments have developed their own production capacity, often under protective policies. However, as long as Canada has rich internal supplies of basic resources, the possibility for larger external trade will continue. If trade barriers against Canadian exports of processed and fabricated resources are removed, this will enhance the logic and effectiveness of government efforts to encourage a greater degree of processing and fabricating in Canadian production and exports. We should be aware, however, that Canada's attainment of processing and fabricating benefits from free trade would also depend on whether governments of other countries discontinued their interventions on behalf of marginal producers.

For petroleum and its products, government interventions are of even greater importance. Import quotas in the United States, export quotas which are implicit in Canada's national energy policy, and state or provincial regulations on production would temper the effects of removing formal trade barriers. Quirin argued that rationalization of controls (which means the elimination of all except those designed to ensure efficient development of oil fields) would increase both the efficiency of production in existing oil fields and the efficient exploration and development of new ones.

The effects of free trade on Canadian refinery activity might be marked. There is a distinct advantage in locating refinery activities near major markets, and although the largest North American markets will of course continue to be in the United States, the existence of a significant number of U.S. refineries just south of the U.S.-Canada border suggests that augmented refinery capacity just north of that border—in Canada—would not be at a noticeable locational disadvantage with free trade in refined products. Moreover, even greater advantages for Canadian refineries could emerge from increased opportunities for export of petrochemical products, especially in the midwest, where U.S. tariffs now present substantial barriers to Canadian exports. It can be assumed that the rationalization of crude oil production in Canada, combined with rising scarcities, instabilities, and costs in other countries, would enable whatever price adjustments were necessary to make petrochemical producers in southern Ontario and southern Quebec more competitive in the Great Lakes area of the United States.

Turning to the steel industry, one finds another interesting situation. The

Canadian industry displayed a remarkable record of import substitution during the latter 1950s, at the very time when the overvaluation of the dollar made imports more attractive than usual. This was basically due to a substantial increase in the size of the Canadian market—owing notably to increased pipeline construction—that made it possible for Canadian producers to attain technologically advanced facilities and economies of scale, especially in rolled products, not previously possible. Adaptations in technology also demonstrated what could be done efficiently on a smaller scale than that familiar to U.S. producers. It is now commonplace to note that Canadian steel prices are generally not higher than those in the United States, where substantial sunk investment in old facilities retards the process of technological advance. Under these circumstances, Canadian producers have little to fear from the normal competition of U.S. firms.

According to Jacques Singer, author of *Trade Liberalization and the Canadian Steel Industry*,[4] the Canadian producers' principal concern in matters affecting international trade in steel lies in the fear of dumping, especially from Japan and Europe. The future growth of Japanese steel exports will depend in part upon the prospect for exports by Japanese steel-using industries, but more importantly on the extent to which export prices may be subsidized by artificially high domestic prices. The problem of artificial pricing is also believed to prevail in Europe, though the specifics of public and private policies vary. Clearly, the experience in steel suggests the need for commitments to control policies which frustrate normal flows of trade and to prevent some suppliers from using the protection arising from transport costs as a possible basis for dumping even under free trade conditions. Singer believes the unanswered question in regard to Japan, even more so than in regard to Europe, is the degree to which that country would be competitive in a setting adhering to North American rules of competitive behaviour. In such a setting, he feels, the Canadian steel industry would be quite able to compete with European producers and perhaps even with Japan.

The only evidence on the textile industry now available is based on earlier studies and on interviews with primary cotton and synthetics producers. Textile manufacturers, especially in cottons, experienced considerable pressure during the late 1950s when the Canadian dollar was overvalued. This resulted in some corporate casualties and the modernization of the larger remaining firms. There is now a feeling that the plant available to these firms could supply the North American market on a competitive basis. However, there is much less confidence about the impact of trade policies that would permit increased imports from low-wage or developing countries, especially

[4]Jacques Singer, *Trade Liberalization and the Canadian Steel Industry*, PPAC series "Canada in the Atlantic Economy," no. 7, Toronto, University of Toronto Press, 1969.

of the less sophisticated textile products. Producers of primary synthetic textiles, being capital-intensive as well as increasingly oriented to sophisticated products, do not, of course, have the same concern. Their principal competitive problem relates to the short runs of many lines and the higher costs of capital equipment. The removal of trade barriers would go far towards removing these problems, enabling Canadian producers to specialize in production of certain lines widely used in North America, while other less common or less sophisticated types produced by low-wage countries could be imported.

The pulp and paper industry, Canada's largest industry in terms of employment, provides a particularly interesting cross-section of Canadian manufacturing industry and its problems. Although, because of its large pulp and newsprint sector, it is frequently identified as a resource industry with an export orientation, the non-newsprint grades have been produced primarily for a domestic market protected by uniformly high tariff barriers. There is considerable product variety within this sector, and some products, such as tissues, are sold under consumer brand names, while others (construction materials, book papers) are purchased primarily as intermediate inputs, and still others (box board and wrapping papers) are widely used throughout industry and trade.

The AESP study of this industry, *Trade Liberalization and the Canadian Pulp and Paper Industry*, by W. E. Haviland, N. S. Takacsy, and E. M. Cape,[5] was not primarily concerned with pulp or newsprint (which are already being produced in Canada under internationally competitive conditions of large scale and high degree of specialization), but with the tariff-protected, small-scale, and product-diversified activity in such grades as fine papers, sanitary tissues, paperboards, and groundwood papers other than newsprint. The comparative-cost part of the analysis employed a hypothetical-mill technique in which equally large and specialized mills were conceived as operating in various Canadian and American regions.

Nordic producers, according to the authors, could not hope to be significant competitors in North America under free trade, except for certain specialty grades, while efficient North American producers could be cost-competitive in Europe, although they would have a long way to go in establishing marketing channels comparable to those possessed by Nordic producers.

In the comparisons between relevant Canadian and U.S. regions, all components of mill costs were estimated in detail, and to these were added

[5]W. E. Haviland *et al., Trade Liberalization and the Canadian Pulp and Paper Industry*, PPAC series "Canada in the Atlantic Economy," no. 5, Toronto, University of Toronto Press, 1969.

hypothetical free trade rail rates and other estimated delivery costs. It was found that the southern region of the United States has a wood-density advantage that results in a wood-cost advantage over eastern Canada in the production of most papers and paperboards. The eastern Canadian producers could offset this with a transport-cost advantage to U.S. market areas down to about a line through New York and Chicago. Eastern Canadian producers would be in about an equal cost position compared with north-central and northeastern U.S. regions, with slight Canadian production-cost advantages being offset by slight U.S. rail-rate advantages.

For eastern Canadian producers, the best lines of specialization under free trade appeared likely to be, first, sanitary tissues, because the southern U.S. region is absent from competition owing to its coarse woods and because a lot of electricity is required and is cheaper in eastern Canada than in north-central and northeastern U.S. regions; second, groundwood papers, which also require a lot of electricity; third, fine papers, where the substantial use of hardwood narrows the density gap between Canadian and southern wood; and last, kraft paperboard and papers, for which southern wood is particularly well suited. However, the relative regional advantages and disadvantages did not differ significantly among the different types of papers and boards.

British Columbia and the U.S. Northwest would be about equally competitive in western North American markets and would also be competitive, since their wood costs are so low, in Atlantic overseas, as well as Pacific overseas, markets.

Marketing problems would undoubtedly be very great for Canadian-owned producers of hitherto tariff-protected grades. For fine papers and some groundwood papers, distribution channels in the United States are predominantly owned or controlled by U.S. paper concerns. Most sanitary tissues are saleable only as brand names, and U.S. producers possess established positions and economies of advertising. In paperboard, producers usually need affiliations with firms that convert paperboard into boxes. For many kinds of paper, Canadian producers, while having to reduce their range of products in order to economize costs, would at the same time have to maintain a sufficient range to interest distributors and buyers.

While effective transitional policies would be vital to any free trade arrangement for Canadian industries, the general case for adjustment assistance applies with special force to the pulp and paper industry, because so many of the mills are located in single-industry communities that could be seriously injured by dislocations; moreover, these single-industry communities are often located in regions that suffer from above-average unemployment rates. Other important policy issues include incentives to logging mechanization, reform of rail-rate and tax-rate structures, assistance in advertising and sales promotion, and questions pertaining to anti-dumping and anti-combines provisions. Provincial governments would be faced with crucial policy questions concerning the financing of forest access roads, the charges and tenure for timber limits, and the public role in reforestation, fire and insect control, and regional development programs.

What has been said about the paper industry seems relevant in important respects to other manufacturing industries, but each has its distinctive characteristics. In chemical industries, there is also product variety and thus the possibility of specialization, but the nature of the technology implies relatively fixed production coefficients for any given level of scale—which may make it more difficult to match demand and supply patterns in a small market. Locational consideration in chemicals also places the main U.S. competition in the south for some products and in the heartland for others, and the costs of many chemicals, including particularly petrochemicals, are affected by the importance of public policies governing production and trade in petroleum. But research and development, and in some lines distribution outlays, are of greater importance. Export markets here provide a basis for development of distinctive Canadian products which it would prove too risky to supply in the quantities required for production economies in the domestic market alone. Something of the same can be said in respect of industrial machinery.

For example, B. W. Wilkinson's study, *Canada's International Trade: An Analysis of Recent Trends and Patterns,*[6] brought some new information to bear on the importance of sales effort and cost factors, as well as R and D factors, in improving the prospects for exports of Canadian industrial machinery. Wilkinson, in investigating selling costs as an influence on foreign trade, showed that such costs were relatively high for consumer goods, but were relatively much lower for investment goods, particularly because mass advertising and distribution are much less important. He also placed emphasis on "aggressiveness" as a factor in exporting investment goods, drawing some of his evidence from a British management study that sorted managements into "sleepers" and "thrusters" according to their attitudes towards market research and exports. In regard to research and development, Wilkinson's statistical correlations, covering 63 secondary manufacturing industries, indicated that a one percent increase in research and development tended to be accompanied by an increase of 0.56 percent in exports as a percentage of output.

Both Wilkinson and English[7] laid stress on human-capital intensiveness

[6]Bruce W. Wilkinson, *Canada's International Trade: An Analysis of Recent Trends and Patterns*, Montreal, Canadian Trade Committee, 1968.
[7]*Ibid.*, and English, *Industrial Structure* ...

(high quality of labour) as a key factor determining the success of manufacturing exports. Wilkinson's finding was derived from statistical correlations for 133 manufacturing industries. English's main point with respect to machinery industries was that for such industries the crucial factor was not so much scale of plant, but rather scale of the engineering and other technical departments in terms of number and quality of people involved. Canada, having an abundance of engineers and other technical people, could achieve much greater export success with machinery products in the absence of trade barriers.

In this era of the auto pact, consumer durables have received more specific attention than other sectors. It is clear that rationalization was required and that integration of the North American industry has improved productivity in the Canadian sector. What is less clear is how far the lessons from the experience of this industry can be applied to other sectors of manufacturing. It is difficult to resist the observation that limitation of such an arrangement to a single industry causes distortions as well as the fundamental political problem of achieving meaningful reciprocity in a single industry. The most vital single issue has centred on the pressures generated in factor markets, especially in the labour market. If wage parity were to promote a movement to commercial and other policy changes in protected sectors now experiencing pressures towards parity as a consequence of the automobile industry's wage trends, then one could scarcely complain; but if the effect of a narrowing wage differential is, instead, merely to reinforce demands for protective policies, sectoral free trade schemes could have a perverse influence.

The most comprehensive and detailed examination of the auto pact undertaken to date has been Carl E. Beigie's 1970 book, *The Canada-U.S. Automotive Agreement: An Evaluation*.[8] Beigie found that efficiency and productivity of the Canadian industry rose markedly as a result of the agreement: from 1964 to 1968, automotive production in Canada expanded three times as fast as employment in the industry. Prior to the agreement, motor vehicles were priced at least 10 percent higher, and employees were paid 30 percent less, than south of the border; by 1968 the price differential for cars had been reduced to about 4 percent, and wages paid by Canadian motor vehicle producers were well on their way towards dollar-for-dollar parity with U.S. wage levels in the industry. By the end of 1968, the conditions and commitments with respect to Canadian production contained in the pact had been overfulfilled by about $400 million. According to Beigie, the productivity gains and cost savings achieved in the Canadian industry were more impor-

[8]Carl E. Beigie, *The Canada-U.S. Automotive Agreement: An Evaluation*, Montreal and Washington, Canadian-American Committee, 1970.

tant than the "safeguards" or specific restrictions to completely free trade in bringing about the striking improvement that took place in Canada's automotive trade balance.

Beigie's view concerning the feasibility of possible attempts to duplicate the automotive agreement in other industrial sectors was that a conflict would be apt to arise if the attempts were addressed in piecemeal fashion to individual sectors. This conflict would stem, he thought, from the inequitable gains, particularly in employment, among the countries that participated in a single-sector arrangement. However, he suggested, it would be possible, through a process of careful selection, to put together a group of industries for which free trade could be mutually beneficial to the participating countries, with gains in some sectors compensating for each country's losses in other sectors. A still better approach, he felt, would be a long-term commitment to North American free trade in all manufactured products, an arrangement that would be particularly beneficial to Canada's overall economic interests.

In any event, a key aspect of the automotive agreement is that it provides the only actual example to date in Canada of the achievements and problems that the country might expect from free trade coupled (unlike the agricultural-machinery case) with transitional mechanisms.

The electrical-apparatus industry, which would appear to qualify for rationalization along lines similar to that in the auto industry, faces a more complex adjustment problem, as noted by English. This is partly because, unlike the auto industry in Canada, the electrical-apparatus firms are not all foreign-owned, so that many would be required to develop new marketing facilities in external markets. Therefore, according to English, it would be desirable to provide for transitional policies that would take account of these different requirements, yet would avoid any techniques for long-term discrimination or subsidy.

A consumer-durables industry that was examined in the Atlantic Economic Studies Program is the furniture industry, frequently regarded as one that would be among the weakest if confronted by trade liberalization. Again, however, generalization is risky, and various product lines are in different situations. These differences and their implications were brought out in the study *Trade Liberalization and the Canadian Furniture Industry*, by David E. Bond and Ronald J. Wonnacott.[9]

A particularly vulnerable segment of the industry, according to the authors,

[9]David E. Bond and Ronald J. Wonnacott, *Trade Liberalization and the Canadian Furniture Industry*, PPAC series "Canada in the Atlantic Economy," no. 6, Toronto, University of Toronto Press, 1968.

would be that which makes casegoods (wooden household furniture) and accounts for the bulk of the industry's business and employment. The numerous Canadian firms are generally small, unduly diversified in their production, undercapitalized, limited in their ability to extend credit to dealers, and lacking in modern equipment and original design. This sector would require mergers, greater emphasis on style, and transitional mechanisms that would include ample financial assistance, if the sector were to have a chance of surviving import competition and seizing export opportunities in the event of free trade. That portion of the industry devoted to local or custom work would not necessarily have to change a great deal, because it would be likely to remain about as immune to lower-priced imports as it has been to lower-priced domestic factory furniture. As for upholstery, bedding, and inexpensive lines of metal furniture, these are partly protected by their weight/value ratios, which make transport costs significant, so that free trade would not be likely to bring a great increase in either imports or exports. But if Canadian producers were able to develop their own designs or to manufacture American or other foreign designs under licence, they might be able to expand their overall operations through sales in urban markets along both sides of the Canada-U.S. border.

Agriculture ought not to be omitted from the discussion, although the difficulties of liberalizing trade in agriculture have traditionally been greater, and the prospects of success lower, than for other products generally. The AESP book *Trade Liberalization and Canadian Agriculture*,[10] published in 1968, contained two separate studies, "The Impact of Trade Liberalization on Canadian Agriculture," by Gerald Trant, and "Prospects for Trade Liberalization in Agriculture," by David MacFarlane and Lewis Fischer.

Trant used a newly developed measure of productivity in showing that, since World War II, Canadian agricultural productivity had increased almost twice as rapidly as that of the United States. He noted that other measures of productivity showed a less dramatic difference, but that all measures led to the conclusion that the Canadian performance in this respect had been better than the American. The main reason, according to the author, was that the United States frequently resorted to high price supports and thus extended the sphere of marginal production, while Canadian agriculture was generally left to adjust to the forces of a relatively free market. Trant's principal question, then, was whether free trade, implying a common pool of technology and the free movement of productive resources between Canada and the United States, would permit Canada's productivity "head start" to

[10]Gerald I. Trant *et al.*, *Trade Liberalization and Canadian Agriculture*, PPAC series "Canada in the Atlantic Economy," no. 4, Toronto, University of Toronto Press, 1968.

be maintained. He concluded that the largest share of Canadian agriculture was concentrated in sectors with the greatest advantages and would be sufficiently competitive to look after itself under free trade. (For example, the important grain crops, which account for more than 50 percent of the value of Canada's agricultural exports, showed a clear-cut advantage that would be retained under free trade.) Meanwhile, very few commodities appeared likely to be at a marked disadvantage under free trade.

Trant's ranking of the strength of Canadian agricultural products under free trade was that the strongest group would include wheat, oats, barley, flax, rapeseed, beef feeder cattle, and purebred dairy cattle; the next-strongest group would include cheddar cheese and specialty pork products; a group for which neither a prospective advantage nor disadvantage could be ascertained included tobacco, grain corn, fresh beef, fresh pork, eggs, soybeans, dried milk powder and fluid milk; products in which Canada seemed likely to have a disadvantage included fruits and vegetables, sugar, poultry meat, butter, mutton, lamb, and wool.

There is no doubt that the less competitive product lines, although they represent a small proportion of total Canadian agriculture, would present almost intractable adjustment problems, largely because of the geographical concentration of agricultural activity and immobility of factors of production. While it cannot be anticipated that Canadian governments will soon favour removing protection of these sectors, it is reasonable to hope that progress in free trade in the non-agricultural products (on which farmers have always felt they were forced by tariffs to pay higher prices) might help to free trade in the agricultural products.

MacFarlane and Fischer pointed out that the United States, the country whose domestic farm programs had been a major barrier to increased trade, had been freeing one farm product after another from some of the most objectionable controls. The experience of the 1960s appeared to have proved conclusively that a procedure of setting price first, and then attempting to adjust output to that price, was not a practicable solution to the problem of farm income. In addition, MacFarlane and Fischer expressed the belief that the developing countries' increasingly urgent need for food aid would sooner or later force the North Atlantic nations to consider seriously the costs of agricultural protectionism in terms of broad international goals as well as of domestic welfare. An increased willingness by the U.S. government to reassess its farm programs would be of great importance in strengthening the hands of those North American agricultural interests that hold a positive attitude towards trade liberalization and wish to encourage some liberalization of domestic agricultural policies in Europe and Japan.

*Regional impacts*

It is appropriate to refer to the regional impacts of free trade, especially since, in an important way, these are consequences of the impacts on industries as examined in the AESP industry studies. Other works discussed in this chapter usually had regional implications, particularly the Wonnacotts' work on free trade in North America, which was essentially a regional analysis.

As part of the AESP program, as well as on behalf of the Economic Council of Canada and the Economic Council of Ontario, T. L. Powrie prepared a background paper in 1969 entitled "Regional Effects of the Canadian Tariff." His analysis was concerned with the tariff's impact (or with the tariff removal's impact) on all the country's major regions, not any particular one. Concurrently with Powrie's undertaking, an in-depth study of free trade's impact on a particular region, British Columbia, was undertaken by Ronald Shearer, John Young, and Gordon Munro and was published in 1971 as *Trade Liberalization and a Regional Economy: Studies of the Impact of Free Trade on British Columbia.*[11] Both Powrie's paper and the study on British Columbia dealt with at least four major concepts for measuring the regional effects of the tariff or its removal:

(1) the "consumption" effect (excess prices to consumers as a result of the tariff, and cheaper procurement as a result of tariff removal);

(2) the "cash cost" of the tariff (protected inefficiency of industry) and the "transfer" effect of removing the tariff and distributing the benefits regionally;

(3) the "increased-export-earnings" effect of removing the tariff (apart from the "reorganization-of-industry" effect that might further increase export earnings);

(4) the "reorganization-of-industry" effect.

Powrie's estimate of the consumer surplus lost to Canada as a consequence of the tariff was $250 million. This is a cost that is shared among regions in the country in accordance with the distribution of consumption expenditure and is therefore a proportionate tax. Powrie did not try to estimate the regional distribution of this cost. For British Columbia, Shearer estimated the figure to be $115 million.

Powrie did try to apportion regionally the effect of the cash cost and its transfer. For Canada as a whole, Powrie estimated the cash cost as $2 billion. The regional effects of removing the tariff would be, according to his calculations, a loss of $300 million to Ontario and of $140 million to Quebec, with

---

[11]Ronald A. Shearer *et al., Trade Liberalization and a Regional Economy: Studies of the Impact of Free Trade on British Columbia,* PPAC series "Canada in the Atlantic Economy," no. 11, Toronto, University of Toronto Press, 1971.

gains to the outlying regions ranging from $80 million for the Atlantic provinces to $220 million for the Prairies. In the Shearer-Young-Munro study, the transfer of the cash cost was estimated to yield a gain of only $60 million to British Columbia.

The latter study estimated British Columbia's gain from increased export earnings (apart from any reorganization-of-industry effect) as $10 million. The three authors of this study, particularly Gordon Munro, who studied closely the question of "stunted" manufacturing, did not feel that the province's scope for major reorganization of manufacturing was considerable, except in certain lines of the paper industry and perhaps in certain areas of mineral processing. They did not try to set a figure on the gains from such possibilities.

Powrie too saw the reorganization effect of tariff removal as likely, for the most part, to be beneficial to Ontario and Quebec, rather than to the outlying regions. He estimated a massive improvement for the two central provinces—$2.75 billion for Ontario and $1.65 billion for Quebec. Because of the concentration of industry with incompletely realized potential in the two central provinces, the "reorganization" plus the "consumption" effects imply gains that would greatly offset the central provinces' "transfer" loss to the outlying provinces and would give the central provinces the largest net gains from free trade of any Canadian region.

Shearer, in noting that the gains from free trade would be proportionately greater for the central provinces than for British Columbia, but that it is easier to mount popular support for free trade in British Columbia, explains this paradox by pointing out that central Canada would require a major restructuring of industry in order to capture the gains from free trade (and this worries some individuals and firms), while the gains are more obvious to, and could be captured more easily by, British Columbians—in the form of higher real income *without* major restructuring. The estimate that the Shearer-Young-Munro study made for the *total* gain to British Columbia from the three effects (not counting any restructuring effect) was $185 million or 5.5 percent of the province's personal income.

*Policy observations*

The role of the government is important in a number of respects in the provision of transitional policies and a general environment favourable to economic growth. The need for transitional assistance does not mean that government need obtain, for each industry, the kind of foreign-parent commitment attached to the Canada-U.S. auto pact. There is a tendency on the part of some government people to underestimate the capacity of industry to make a rational response to the simple incentive of tariff removal. But policy lessons do emerge from the study of a variety of specific industries, and the following inferences are cited as leading examples:

1. A predictable commercial-policy environment is of great importance—many manufacturers prefer the establishment of a general free trade association rather than any alternative option, precisely because a general free trade area would enable investment planning to be based on a climate of certainty and because, being embodied in a treaty arrangement, it would reduce the danger of backsliding.

2. Manufacturers are greatly concerned with costs of inputs. This often means great skepticism regarding sector deals that inevitably fail to take account of important protected materials and components. Again, this factor favours the general or uniform approach to trade liberalization—through either a comprehensive multilateral arrangement or a free trade area.

3. The importance of non-tariff barriers in some industries also tends to support the free-trade-association approach, since these barriers frequently relate to domestic policies, such as public purchasing policies or policies governing direct foreign investment, which cannot readily be brought into multilateral negotiations of the traditional kind.

4. Among transitional problems (apart from the clear necessity of a transition period for reinvestment), the most important ones probably relate to marketing and, to a lesser extent, research and development. Firms need time and also perhaps some aids to information flows that will place them on a competitive basis vis-à-vis long-established firms. This especially affects Canadian firms attempting to compete with international companies based in the United States. The problem in research and development activity is less serious, because acquisition of technology is not difficult. Here the need is for a market base adequate to enable Canadian firms or subsidiaries to exploit on more equal terms the international technology pool and to develop and market distinctive Canadian products.

These observations relate primarily to the adjustment process. It cannot be too strongly stated that it is the fear of the adjustment, rather than any deep fear of the ultimate outcome, that most stands in the way of acceptance of a bold policy, based on trade liberalization, for rationalizing industry. Senior officials of both private industry and government might go along with political leadership in such a program if they were confident that the political leaders could stomach adjustment and could identify and adopt appropriate transitional policies. From the standpoint of overcoming political inertia, the best argument for industry studies may be that they identify, at the level of industrial detail, the varied elements of adjustment required.

# 6. The Adjustment Mechanism and its Operation under Trade Liberalization

The discussion in the previous chapter focused on particular industrial sectors or regions and their prospects for meeting international competition. It was necessary there, implicitly or explicitly, to make certain simplifying assumptions. Most important, we have assumed that the "average" competitive position of the Canadian economy, as reflected in the value of the Canadian dollar relative to other currencies, remained constant, This is the only practical assumption to make when dealing with any particular industry. Only when one has examined a large proportion of such sectors, or at least a sufficiently representative group, is it possible to have a clear idea of the probability of an improved competitive position for the entire domestic economy relative to the world economy. Presumably, if most industries proved, after an appropriate transition period, to be stronger relative to similar industries in other countries after trade barriers were removed than before, then the competitive position of the economy in general could also be expected to improve, and thus should be reflected in some general adjustment of Canada's position in the world economy.

The most obvious change that might occur as a result of an improved Canadian competitive position would be a rise in the value of the Canadian dollar. But to approach the question of appropriate adjustment more systematically, it is well to consider first a kind of change that might moderate or even eliminate the exchange-rate adjustment required. This is the relationship between international capital flows and changes in commodity trade. Only if changes in capital movements do not compensate for changes in trade flows will there be need for a monetary adjustment—in the exchange rate or comparative price levels. We shall consider these in turn and then come back to the question of adjustment in individual industrial sectors at the end of the chapter.

*The role of capital movements in Canada's international adjustment process*

According to economic theory, capital movements can be expected to help the national development process to complement shifting trade patterns so as to reduce the need for substantial changes in exchange values. This complementary role of capital movements can be illustrated as follows: When a country is at an early stage of development, it will not have great productive capacity, so it will not be able to export very much and must import to supply many of its needs. Thus, it is likely to have a considerable deficit on commodity trade. However, if its development potential is great (and other conditions such as political stability are present), capital will be attracted from more developed nations, and this will enable the country to sustain a trade deficit and to develop more quickly. Later, as the developing country expands its production and hence its export capacity, the relative importance of foreign capital may decline and a substantial export surplus may be generated, with part of the proceeds from this surplus going to the interest and dividend payments that the developing country must make to those in other countries who had supplied foreign capital in the past. Still later in the development process, a country may sustain its surplus of merchandise exports over imports by becoming a net capital exporter itself. This is a very simplified description of the complementary role that capital and commodity movements may play in the development process. How relevant are they to the explanation of Canadian experience, particularly in recent years?

There is a substantial literature on the application of basic balance of payments concepts to Canada, starting with the classic work by Viner on Canada's balance during the early years of this century. It is not appropriate or necessary to review this literature here. The most relevant conclusions for our purposes are that economic forces have predominated in explaining Canada's balance of international payments and that Canada has seldom experienced significant balance of payments difficulties arising out of its high degree of dependence upon international markets. In those instances where international events have had a massive impact, as during the depressions and wars, it is possible to imagine that Canada might have benefited from a comfortable isolation. But even in these circumstances there would have been a serious loss of growth potential from isolation. In more normal conditions of prosperity in the world economy, such as have generally prevailed during the past two decades, it is totally unrealistic to expect that any benefits Canada might derive from significantly reducing its degree of integration with the world economy could begin to compensate for the income foregone. The leading industrial powers, recognizing interdependence, have sought to resolve the problems of protectionism and monetary instability by direct attack through improvement of international institutions. Each individual country should assess its own performance relative to that of these institutions and of the national governments of its main trading partners; it can then decide in a more realistic context whether its performance would be improved by lessening its degree of international dependence and by increasing the scope for national authorities to be free of international market and institutional disciplines.

The record of Canadian experience during the 1950s and early 1960s has been examined by Caves and Reuber for the *Canada in the Atlantic Economy* series.[1] Their work has been supplemented by application of the same methodology to the rest of the 1960s.[2] This research has thrown light on a number of aspects of the role of international capital flows in Canada. For the purposes of this chapter, the most important conclusions are the following:

1. The inflow of short-term and portfolio capital into Canada has been responsive to changes in interest-rate differentials between Canada and the United States, and direct investment has been responsive to changes in Canadian GNP and exports. These relationships largely reflect the strength of economic growth forces, especially in the 1950s, and the highly integrated operation of the North American capital market.

2. The flow of direct investment and of some portfolio investment is classed as autonomous in the sense that it is not primarily motivated by balance of payments, exchange-rate, or other monetary considerations. In the Canadian case, direct investment has clearly been a response to improved growth potentials and has been largely requited by imports of goods and services, so that it has generated little or no disturbance in the overall balance of payments. In this and other respects, such direct capital has been complementary to domestic investment and has contributed to a more rapid rate of real growth and a higher volume of exports than would otherwise have occurred. Inflows of portfolio capital, however, have not been so fully requited by other factors; and when this type of inflow has been dominant, the Canadian dollar has tended to appreciate above levels expected on other grounds.

3. Short-term capital flows appear to have responded to monetary factors in a stabilizing way, except for periods when changes in the exchange rate in one direction were clearly expected—e.g., in 1950, when the Canadian dollar was undervalued following the devaluation of 1949, and in 1961,

[1]Richard E. Caves and Grant L. Reuber, *Canadian Economic Policy and the Impact of International Capital Flows*, PPAC series "Canada in the Atlantic Economy," no. 10, Toronto, University of Toronto Press, 1969. The same authors also published a more extended book, *Capital Transfers and Economic Policy: Canada 1951–62*, in Harvard Economic Studies 135, Cambridge, Massachusetts, 1971.
[2]Richard E. Caves and Grant L. Reuber, "International Capital Markets and Canadian Economic Policy under Flexible and Fixed Exchange Rates, 1952–69," Research Report 7125, Department of Economics, University of Western Ontario.

when it appeared that the government was anxious to see the currency depreciated. Both these situations could be, and were, remedied by Canadian policy changes.

4. Comparison of the periods of flexible exchange rates (the 1950s) with the period of a fixed rate (the 1960s) is made difficult by substantial changes in the international environment, particularly the coming of convertibility of European currencies and the increasingly apparent need for a change in the exchange relationship between the U.S. dollar and the currencies of the main overseas industrial powers. Because of these developments, the international pattern of interest rates and capital flows in the 1960s was the result of a more complex set of relationships than it was in the 1950s. However, while this makes the interpretation of the statistical record for Canada more difficult, Caves and Reuber did not find that capital movements played a markedly different role during the two periods. The difference that did appear can be attributed in part (perhaps largely) to changes in the extent of interventions by the U.S. government.

5. One area that warrants special attention is the effect of capital flows on the leverage that can be achieved by the Canadian government with monetary and fiscal policies. Caves and Reuber found some support in Canada's postwar experience for the claim that monetary policy is more effective under a flexible-exchange-rate policy, whereas fixed rates give fiscal policy a larger relative role. However, they qualify this in the case of deficit fiscal policy, because of the monetary consequences arising out of debt financing. Observation of these policy effects has also been influenced by special considerations—the perverse use of monetary policy in the late 1950s under a flexible exchange system and the rather heavier reliance on monetary than on fiscal policy in the period 1968 to 1970 under a fixed-exchange-rate system. One forms the overall impression that, for aggregate policy choices, differences between exchange systems have been less important than variations in national and international policy in explaining changes in the role of international capital movements in Canada in the past twenty years. One falls back on one fundamental position favouring the flexible-rate system: "When the incidence of disturbances is so great, and the predictability of the economic system's responses to policy actions so poor, good policy marksmanship in the political setting of western democracies becomes in practice impossible. J. E. Meade's argument for flexible exchange rates as a means of conserving scarce policy instruments appears to be as applicable now as ever."[3]

Looking to the future, one can expect that the decline in Canada's rela-

[3]Caves and Reuber, Research Report 7125, p. 27.

tive position as a recipient of long-term international capital will continue and also that Canada will continue to grow as a supplier of long-term capital through private investment and foreign aid. Under these circumstances, the importance of policies for encouraging or restricting the size of foreign-capital inflows into Canada will diminish. Particular needs will still exist for foreign capital in individual industries—or perhaps more particularly for the kind of package of managerial skills that so often goes along with foreign capital in the establishment of new industries. But the serving of this need may well be compatible with a more restrictive general attitude to new foreign-capital imports.

The actual outcome will depend most significantly upon the future strength of the current account. There is no doubt that this account has been strong in recent years, although the near-term outlook may be affected by the growing imports usually associated with a period of expansion in Canada. The early chapters of this study, especially the estimates in Chapter 4, indicate that trade liberalization should mean a continued strong current account. Even the least optimistic of these projections suggest that a relatively modest level of capital inflow would take care of this aspect of the balance of payments adjustment. The adjustment of Canada's industrial structure in response to free trade, however, is another matter. Given the importance of the rationalization process that would be necessary and the particular significance of this for industries where foreign ownership is common, it seems likely that the initial effect of a move to free trade would be to generate a substantial capital transfer by firms engaged in industrial restructuring. Since this would be a transitional phenomenon that might exacerbate the adjustment problems under flexible exchange rates, it might be desirable to neutralize its exchange-rate effects. To the extent that such inflow was requited by capital-goods (or other) imports during the transition (as during the 1950s), however, this exchange-rate effect could be avoided.

*Monetary and price adjustments*

Instead of, or in addition to, capital flows, there can be more purely monetary adjustments—either through factor pricing or through the exchange rate. The actual pattern of adjustment depends on the flexibility of various elements in the price mechanism. Clearly, most factor prices are rather inflexible, especially in the downward direction. This is particularly true for industrial materials and skilled labour. To the extent that the adjustment to free trade improves productivity, it is quite likely that this will result in higher wages. It is noteworthy that Canada's export industries are among those that pay the highest wages. But under circumstances of vigorous import competition, the nature of the dispersion effects of wage improvements may change. In the past, high wages in export industries have probably pulled up wages in those protected industries that were able to pay high wages primarily because of the profits of protection. Under free trade, some of these protected industries would be unable to afford to pay higher wages, so the effect of pressures on factor markets should be a more rapid transfer of resources to export industries and to those sectors able to compete most effectively with imports.

With fixed exchange rates, the overall or average effect of the changed competitive position of each national economy should be reflected in a new pattern of exchange relationships, unless all countries experience similar growth stimuli. However, the immediate effect of adjustment under a fixed exchange rate would be to alter foreign-exchange reserves. If they were to be sharply depleted during the period of transition, it is likely that devaluation would be necessary. Alternatively, if foreign-exchange reserves were to build up as a consequence of the improved "average" competitive position of any national economy, this might not lead to a revaluation, on grounds that it could prove to be a temporary situation. In this case, however, those industries showing a marked improvement in their international competitive strength might well be under such pressure for wage increases that the under-valuation of the currency would result in larger wage or other factor-price improvements that would not have occurred during the transition period if the value of the currency had been allowed to appreciate. Of course, if the long-run trend were in an upward direction, these improvements would constitute a mere anticipation, or earlier realization, of the gains from free trade, at least for the fortunate factors of production.

The main advantage of allowing exchange-rate flexibility is that it spreads the benefits of free trade to all members of the community, rather than allo-cating a larger portion of them to those who are able to exert more effective upward pressure on their incomes. It also permits an easy adjustment to transition and post-transition phases of the move to free trade, without any need for explicit agreement on changes in currency values during the adjust-ment period. This is an almost ideal system, provided that the fluctuations in exchange values are not so great as to generate new uncertainties in inter-national transactions.

Fears of permitting such an adjustment through exchange-rate flexibility arise in large part out of the difficulty of predicting how great these rate movements might be. An effort has been made in Chapter 4 to estimate the size of the overall adjustment on varying assumptions concerning the static and dynamic effects of trade liberalization. The summary recorded there of *static* effects on Canada's merchandise trade balance is as follows:

(1)  a Canada-U.S. free trade area: plus $50 million to −$130 million;
(2)  Canada, the United States, and EFTA:           ⎫
(3)  Canada, the United States, Japan, Australia,   ⎬  −$75 million to
     and New Zealand:                               ⎭  −$200 million;
(4)  number 3 without the United States: −$40 million to −$60 million;
(5)  number 3 plus EFTA and EEC: −$480 million.

As is explained in Chapter 4, these are pessimistic estimates of the balance of trade effects for Canada, because they are based on the application of price elasticities to 1966 trade levels without allowing for any of the dynamic effects of adjustment to free trade—economies of scale realized by Canadian industry through better access to U.S. and other markets, improved performance of management under international competitive pressures, etc. As Canada is one of the smaller and more protected economies in any of the prospective groupings, there is no doubt that more such dynamic benefits from trade liberalization are available to it than to its prospective trading partners. Given the convenient location of most Canadian industry near the world's richest market, and the now substantial size of the central Canadian market itself, one might confidently anticipate substantial absolute and relative improvements in average Canadian productivity, which should tend to create pressures for an appreciation of the dollar.

All in all, taking the estimates in Chapter 4 of the static balance of payments consequences of the various options, the maximum depreciation that would occur in the Canadian dollar from the free trade alternatives discussed would be between zero and 4 percent; when dynamic considerations are added, the greater probability is for a moderate appreciation above the late 1970 and 1971 level of about 98 cents (U.S.). To the extent that factor-price adjustments also occur, these are likely to limit appreciation but, because of the downward rigidity of many factor prices, are less likely to dampen any depreciation in the exchange rate.

### "Hard-core" adjustment problems

The foregoing seems to be in keeping with the basic evidence on the competitive position and potential for Canadian industry as reported in studies by the Wonnacotts,[4] by Wilkinson,[5] and by those who have examined individual Canadian industries for this series. Yet there appears to be a lingering

[4]Ronald J. Wonnacott and Paul Wonnacott, *Free Trade Between the United States and Canada: The Potential Economic Effects*, Cambridge, Massachusetts, Harvard University Press, 1967.
[5]B. W. Wilkinson, *Canada's International Trade: An Analysis of Recent Trends and Patterns*, Montreal, Canadian Trade Committee, 1968.

doubt about the capacity of the Canadian economy to compete in the context of free trade with the United States and with its other principal trading partners. It is difficult to avoid attributing some of this doubt to an unreasoning fear of competition from large American concerns—a fear nurtured during a long period when the conditions of competition were unequal, largely because of the trade policies adopted by both countries. As the Wonnacotts have emphasized, in the absence of such barriers the exchange rate would itself set limits to the extent to which large shifts in resources would occur in the industrial sector. However, a suspicion also exists in many minds that the adjustment process itself may be beset by difficulties and institutional considerations that could bias the outcome in a direction that is much less favourable to Canada's interests than the "pure" economic analysis of the situation would suggest. This is partly the consequence of the uncertainty shrouding the adjustment process. It is also partly the consequence of the peculiar institutional factors believed to be present in the Canadian-U.S. trade relationship.

The former consideration—uncertainty of adjustment—is subject to policy treatment of the kind proposed by Roy Matthews in his study, *Industrial Viability in a Free Trade Economy.*[6] Essentially, what Matthews is saying is that uncertainty can be minimized by pacing the rate of adjustment so that it can be effectively managed without unnecessary short-term disruption and by spreading the costs so that they are not borne only by those who are directly affected by the changing policy environment. It is not necessary here to summarize the array of policies that might be made available to assist adjustment. Past experience, particularly in the European Economic Community, suggests that the adjustment process may require less government intervention than might be expected in advance. Nevertheless, it may be well to err on the side of excessive adjustment assistance, if only to reduce the political resistance to acceptance of the trade-policy changes leading to adjustment. The adjustment-assistance provisions of the U.S. Trade Expansion Act of 1962 have proven to be rather ungenerous, so demanding are the conditions required to qualify for financial aid.

But it is not the normal uncertainties of adjustment that appear to generate the most serious reservations about Canada's prospects under free trade. It is the fear of the decision pattern that would arise out of the prevalence of foreign-owned enterprises in the Canadian economy. Once the free flow of goods both ways across the Canadian border is possible, it is feared that many head offices will allow their Canadian branches to dwindle into relative

[6]Roy A. Matthews, *Industrial Viability in a Free Trade Economy: A Program of Adjustment Policies for Canada*, PPAC series "Canada in the Atlantic Economy," no. 12, Toronto, University of Toronto Press, 1971.

insignificance. While not formally abandoning their capital, they may make most new investments on the U.S. side and supply the Canadian market increasingly from external sources. Apparently, according to this view of the long-term trend, the U.S. locations will always be either superior or only marginally inferior, and so the incentive to share productive capacity on a more balanced proportional basis between Canada and the United States would be weak.

This pessimistic view of Canada's prospects under free trade is possibly a convenient way of minimizing the risks to bureaucrats and politicians to whom a bold policy may pose a later problem of explaining embarrassing consequences ascribed—though not necessarily attributable—to that action. It is also comforting to that part of the business elite whose autonomy in Canada would be seriously challenged by the requirements of the rationalization process. But it is not economically sound. In the first place, it is, as already suggested, impossible for the adjustment mechanisms to accommodate so one-sided an investment pattern. Secondly, locational economies would favour Canadian plants in all those industries for which a plant of efficient size could dispose of its products primarily within Canada—unless, of course, Canadian resource or labour costs are higher. The size of the Canadian market is repeatedly neglected by the more pessimistic observers. For example, such people sometimes compare Canada with Scotland, thereby failing to take into account that both population and per capita income are substantially greater in Canada.

There is also much oversimplification concerning the size of scale economies at the plant level. The size of the Canadian market, indeed of the Ontario and western Quebec market, is sufficient to absorb the output of one or more plants of minimum efficient scale in most lines of manufacturing activity for which a substantial market exists. Only for highly specialized manufactured products is the Canadian market base likely to be inadequate. For commonly used products, many plants prosper in the United States in submarkets smaller than that of central Canada. That Canada should not get its share of such plants under free trade is to suggest a willingness on the part of industry to deny itself the advantages of transport cost savings, a view that is quite unrealistic.

A more controversial point concerns the alleged disadvantage of Canada as a locus for head offices of international businesses operating in a North American or wider free trade grouping. This disadvantage rests primarily upon the desirability of spreading marketing, product-design, and industrial-research costs. These costs are said to favour the multi-plant firm. It should be stressed that this concern is not basically the same as the argument about plant location, since no matter where the marketing and research activity is conducted, production should still be governed by a largely separable set of locational considerations. The important questions concern the importance of non-plant economies and whether they are likely to favour non-Canadian firms under a free trade arrangement to a greater degree than at present.

To summarize briefly the literature on the first question, one can say that marketing costs are important for a substantial range of consumer products, while research and product-design costs are important for a more limited range of consumer products (especially the durables and some chemicals) and for certain types of capital equipment—e.g., aircraft, military hardware, computers, and some categories of chemicals (e.g., primary plastics). The question is often discussed as though aircraft and military hardware were typical. Even in these industries, however, Canada has achieved some industrial development through a mixture of defence sharing and international business-production allocation. These activities have had to be based on the international market because both production and marketing and research economies have given the international enterprise a clear edge.

For other sectors, however, it has been possible to separate the locus of design and marketing control from plant location. Sometimes this has been done within the enterprise and sometimes by licensing arrangements between enterprises, with the larger, often foreign, enterprise providing the product, and the local enterprise controlling production. In still other instances, both firm and plant economies have been achieved by the Canadian-based firm. Not surprisingly, this has occurred most often where the firm has had free access to international markets. The fundamental lesson to be derived from all of this is that where economies of scale are important to the firm (whether to the plant or not), it will usually be essential for Canadian-based enterprises to operate on the same terms of access to international markets as the other international enterprises with which they must compete.

The object of a policy to ensure the maximum advantages to Canadian-based enterprises must, under these circumstances, be to combine free trade with incentives for Canadian-based enterprises (whether foreign-owned or not) to develop and supply distinctive products to international markets. This would require industrial-research incentives that reward success in areas where Canadian enterprise might be expected to have reasonably good competition prospects. It might also be desirable to consider policies that penalize wasteful marketing activities that contribute to unnecessarily large-scale facilities in some consumer industries, and also to an unnecessary degree of marketing control by established (often foreign) enterprises.

If policies such as the above were instituted in connection with the establishment of a free trade area, it seems probable that most of the feared institutional problems of adjustment to free trade could be avoided. However, given the expected benefits of free trade, further guarantees might also be contemplated, if only on the grounds that they would be worthwhile if they succeeded in counteracting the fears that would otherwise stand in the way of a sound national policy based on trade liberalization. The belief that it is important to have a Canadian head office to supervise Canadian production facilities within an international enterprise and, hopefully, to encourage Canadian design activity might warrant an incentive system rewarding increases in activity measured by output and employment and penalizing the reduction of the ex-factory work force below a certain percentage of the factory work force based upon the ratio between these groups in the parent firm. This is merely illustrative of the kind of guarantee that should encourage a reasonably integrated Canadian branch operation within an international enterprise.

In conclusion, the adjustment of the Canadian economy to free trade is not likely to prove very difficult in the aggregate. The major concern is that policy be directed to avoiding the fear of adjustment, to spreading the cost of adjustment, and to devising guidelines and incentives to minimize difficulties arising out of the role of foreign-owned enterprise in Canada and to exercise control over the investment pattern that would emerge in a North American free trade area. The problems associated with adjustments to competition from other trading partners in any larger grouping are not dissimilar, but they may require fewer uniquely Canadian policy moves, because the impact of European or Japanese exports upon Canada will require adjustment policies largely parallel to those adopted by the United States.

An area of policy that remains to be discussed is that of policy harmonization in areas not so directly related to industrial reorganization, and it is to this that the next chapter is directed.

# 7. The Harmonization of Non-Tariff Economic Policies in a Free Trade Area

*Introduction*

THE AIMS OF ECONOMIC POLICY

In the formulation of economic policies, governments take into consideration foreign economic conditions and the policies that foreign governments are following in order to reach their own goals. The weight of these factors in decisions depends on the extent to which the domestic economy responds to foreign influences. This dependence varies among countries and over time as a function of the size of the domestic economy relative to that of other countries, the size of its foreign-trade sector, the ease with which capital and labour move in and out of the country, and the extent to which its methods and type of production are tied to those of other countries.

The fact that a government's policies respond to foreign conditions and policies does not necessarily mean that the policies of different countries will be complementary to each other. In fact, over most of history, governments attempted to frustrate each other's aims in a type of economic warfare that was very costly to all sides. However, when goals are held in common by a number of countries, usually those that are closely associated by ties of trade and factor movements, the policies may become coordinated in such a way that the effects of a country's own policies and of those of foreign governments tend in the same direction. The policies may differ, but they promote the reaching of goals that are mutually desired. A further stage may arise, for which the term "harmonization" is reserved, which consists of pursuing common goals by the same policies. In other words, the governments of the several countries behave with respect to those policies that are harmonized as if they were one government. This requires consultation, trust, and community of views.

Governments may harmonize only some or few policies and remain independent or only loosely coordinated with respect to the majority of their economic activities. Some policies are obviously easier to harmonize than others, in the sense that the idiosyncrasies of the different societies that are represented by the governments are likely to vary between fields.

THE ADVANTAGES OF HARMONIZATION

The overriding responsibility of governments is for the welfare of the nation rather than that of a group of nations or of the world as a whole. Governments intervene massively in the domestic economy, partly to control overall demand, partly to finance or supply public goods and services, partly to transfer income among individuals, and to some extent to control the structure of industry and the behaviour of firms. But this intervention has repercussions on trade, transfer of income, and the movement of capital and even of populations between countries. Hence, the degree of success of even the best national policies depends in part on foreign economic conditions, and these are affected by the policies of other governments.

Gains in economic efficiency from harmonizing non-tariff governmental policies are the greater the closer are the economic relationships between countries. Thus, the harmonization problem looms ever larger in the modern world of low transport costs, mobility of factors, and good communications. Tariff reductions unify markets and increase trade and so contribute to the importance of harmonizing other governmental policies.

The ordinary tourist can appreciate how much more closely integrated is the international economy now than it was only ten or fifteen years ago, and he can observe the consequences that this change has had on the co-ordination and harmonization of policy. When balance of payments controls and tariffs were higher, it was possible to find articles in some countries that were markedly less expensive than in others. Today, bargains are no longer to be had in advanced economic countries, because international competition forces the prices of producers in different countries into equality and even brings about a much greater similarity of tax rates on particular products. Domestic policies, in consequence, have larger effects abroad and may elicit countervailing action—hence the need to bring national policies into co-ordination and possibly harmonization. International cooperation is needed both to achieve goals that may be held in common and to check the unwanted international repercussions of domestic policy.

The gains from harmonizing some other policies would be greater if tariff policies were harmonized by the creation of area or world free trade, as is envisaged in the studies of which this volume forms a part. But benefits from harmonizing other policies exist without free (or freer) trade. The economic policies of advanced countries are already coordinated to a considerable degree and are to some extent harmonized. Further coordination and harmonization would be designed to reduce distortions and to make international economic relations more efficient.

LIMITATIONS TO HARMONIZATION

The dominant views of different societies as to the appropriateness of different policies for efficiency, full employment, or justice may very well vary in detail, if not in general conception. Different governments may also need different policies because domestic conditions vary among countries, because the incidence of the same policies may vary owing to differences in structure, or because of constitutional or other limitations.

Governments may be faced with conflicts between, on the one hand, co-ordinating or harmonizing policies with those of other countries in order to reach common goals and, on the other hand, the wish to maintain freedom of action in the use of the same policy instruments in order to reach independent goals. These conflicts may arise because one instrument can affect more than one goal or, alternatively, because of the "package-deal" nature of certain agreements. Thus, in the former case, an agreement to bind tariffs for the sake of long-term efficiency in the allocation of resources would prevent the altering of tariffs for short-term balance of payments purposes. The problem of conflicts arising because of the package-deal nature of the ar-rangements is illustrated by the difficulties faced by some of the potential applicants for membership in the European Economic Community. Certain of these countries are attracted by the preferential free trade aspect of the large community and would join it if they could on these grounds, but they are repelled by certain other aspects of EEC policies that are tied to the entire arrangement. Thus Switzerland would clearly wish to join the EEC if all that were involved were membership in the customs union, but the Swiss cannot bring themselves to apply for membership because of the clauses in the pro-spective agreement that would require Switzerland to allow free immigration of labour from other member countries.

OPTIMAL POLICY FOR SMALL COUNTRIES

The problem of policy harmonization is that of determining the extent to which economic policies should be identical or similar in countries that are closely related by trade and capital movements. The purpose of such har-monization is to avoid international patterns of production, trade, and con-sumption that are determined by differences in policy rather than by fundamental economic factors of comparative advantage.

Since a small country can have only a minor influence in determining common policies either for international coordination or in a process of harmonization, its choice tends to be either to accede to the pattern of policies determined by its major trading partner (or partners) or to sacrifice the advantages of coordination and harmonization. To a greater extent than for a more important country, a small country is likely to harmonize on the basis of policies other than those it would have chosen independently.

Maximizing the independence required by a small country for the pursuit of policies suited to its own conditions, rather than to those of others, makes necessary the development of a set of policies in which the sphere of harmonization is minimized. This implies a decentralized system in which the market is interposed as much as possible between the small country and its economic partners. An internationally decentralized system based on the market gives the greatest scope to the pursuit of the small country's own goals, without sacrificing the advantage of economic integration in a wider community. To put this point in another way, a government, like an individual, on the weaker end of a power relationship should rely as much as possible on the impersonal functioning of free markets to manage its relationships with other entities.

A flexible rate of foreign exchange can be seen in this light—as an instrument whereby a country can maintain some independence in economic policy, in order to pursue domestic needs, while at the same time remaining integrated in the international economic community. With a flexible rate, changes in the price level are freed of the necessity to follow changes in the foreign price level; and monetary policy, while still not capable of greatly affecting interest rates, affects the quantity of money and the exchange rate and so can operate to maintain full employment more successfully than is the case in neighbouring countries. The adoption of a flexible exchange rate by Canada to combat world deflationary influences in the 1930s and inflation in the 1950s (and again in 1970) indicates a practical appreciation of this point.

TOWARDS HARMONIZATION

In the past, the main efforts to coordinate and harmonize policies internationally have been in the fields of tariff reductions and balance of payments practices. These measures have led to a generally low level of protection in advanced countries (except for agriculture), to regional customs unions and free trade areas, and to agreement about the need to harmonize policies affecting the balances of payments of countries in such a way as to aid and permit mutual support in overall matters of short-term macro-economic policy.

The remainder of this chapter will discuss the extent to which main policies, other than the tariff, should be coordinated or harmonized so as to eliminate those factors that make prices diverge from real costs and that distort the direction and extent of international trade and capital movements. In addition to balance of payments policies, governmental taxes and expenditures may contribute to inefficiency. There are many other factors that can have similar effects. We will consider the following: policies with respect to the maintenance of competition, including discriminatory behaviour by governments; policies affecting transportation and regional development; and non-tariff barriers to trade. Policies necessary to ease a transition from protection to complete area or world free trade will also be taken up.

## The harmonization of balance of payments policies

There has been great progress in international coordination and harmonization of policies affecting balances of payments since 1936 and especially since the end of the last war. The evolution of international arrangements includes the following results:
(1) the partial demonetization of gold through the segregation of the gold reserves of central banks from the free world gold market;
(2) the resulting dominance of the U.S. dollar as virtually the sole reserve asset, to which are added modest amounts of Special Drawing Rights, a sort of international fiat money;
(3) the possible emergence in the next decade of a competing European reserve currency.

Despite the substantial international collaboration in this field in the past, recent international monetary disturbances clearly demonstrate that more is needed. At present, for example, the total supply of international money is determined virtually by accident. It is the result not only of the U.S. balance of payments deficit, but of all sorts of multilateral and bilateral arrangements, including swap agreements, which give rise to a total supply that is unplanned. Thus more harmonization of balance of payments policies is needed. A future evolution in the direction of free trade areas or general free trade would increase the intimacy of the contact among the economies of major countries and thereby bring about a greater need for clarity about the role and supply of reserves. But these developments would not make a qualitative change in the need for a logical and clear system, which is very pressing in any case.

The international harmonization and coordination of balance of payments policies in most of the advanced countries presently takes place within an elaborate and evolving framework of international institutions, practices, and agreements. The basic institution is the International Monetary Fund, which provides short-term financing of balance of payments deficits and makes possible international consultation about policies affecting balances of payments within a system of essentially fixed rates of exchange. The IMF is supplemented by bilateral arrangements between the major industrialized countries and multilaterally through the Organisation for Economic Co-operation and Development and the Bank for International Settlements.

These balance of payments policies provide an illustration of the need to distinguish between two types or degrees of problem. At one level is the coordination and harmonization necessary to achieve efficiency in world production and consumption, while at another is that additional degree of harmonization that is required on occasion to keep a particular economic system from breaking down from its own inherent contradictions. The weakness of the IMF system is that it harmonizes exchange-*reserve* policies insufficiently, as shown above, and harmonizes exchange-*rate* policies too much by encouraging inflexible rates, as discussed below.

An economic system must have the mechanism to bring to equality the receipts and the payments between the units composing it, be they households, regions, or nations. This is the "adjustment problem." If a disturbance occurs and causes a payments deficit or surplus between the units, be it owing to changes in productivity, borrowing and lending, tastes, price levels, or anything else, some mechanism must eventually be brought into play to restore balance of payments equilibrium. For households or regions, the decrease or accumulation of cash balances and other assets soon causes a reduction or increase in the expenditures of the unit to correct the imbalance.

With the present internationally harmonized system of fixed exchange rates under the International Monetary Fund, the long-run adjustment process among countries takes place similarly in principle to that among households or regions through income and price reductions in deficit countries and increases in surplus countries. But this mechanism is slow in working and unpleasant, especially for deficit countries. A country with a balance of payments deficit is one that is earning less from the sale of goods and services and securities than it is spending and investing abroad. The solution is, then, to decrease its purchases or increase its sales abroad. This can be accomplished, if it is at full employment, only by decreasing consumption or investment.

Whatever the technique to accomplish this decline in domestic command over goods and services, be it fiscal-monetary policy or controls, the result is necessarily painful, since it means that someone consumes or invests less than would otherwise have been the case—hence the typical difficulty of correcting balance of payments deficits rapidly and the lengthiness of the program. Unlike individuals or regions, countries normally can and do resist downward pressures on their command over goods and services, because they control their own money supplies. At the same time, they typically resort to extensive borrowing and eventually to exchange control in order to finance or control the excess of their international expenditures over receipts in the hope that the balance of payments deficit will correct itself in the long run without their having to suffer the full weight of the adjustment mechanism implied in a fixed-exchange-rate system.

Surplus countries coordinate their policies with those of deficit countries in the sense that they make loans to the latter, either formally or by accumulating reserves of foreign currencies, and do not retaliate against exchange controls. These responses are motivated by a desire to avoid a breakdown in the international system such as occurred in the 1930s and also to some extent by the fact that a creditor position confers political power. But the consequence of running a surplus and of accumulating reserves is to put inflationary pressure on incomes and prices of the surplus country. This is harmonization at another and, in part, unwilling level. Even a country that offsets the inflationary monetary effect of an accumulation of reserves on its domestic price level is subject to a direct inflationary influence if prices rise abroad and the exchange rate is fixed. The prices of export and import goods and services rise, and this eventually causes an increase in the prices of home goods that are substitutes in production or consumption for the traded goods. A country cannot prevent its domestic price level from following foreign inflation unless its own economic weight dominates the world price level. The latter is the case only of the United States; the position of Canada is very different. When the exchange rate is fixed, whatever the level of domestic demand and of employment in Canada, the price level must inevitably change parallel to that of the United States.

Imported inflation in the surplus countries is hard to fight through the independent exercise of monetary policy. The integration of capital markets of advanced countries is so close, both directly and through the Euro-dollar market, that individual countries have lost a large part of their power to influence domestic interest rates. This is shown by the parallel movement of rates in major financial markets, even when such movements are unfavourable in the explicit opinion of the monetary authorities of some of them. Calculations of the elasticity of international capital flows and of the transmission of foreign interest-rate changes to Canada demonstrate a great and growing dependence of the Canadian capital market on foreign monetary conditions. Attempts to tighten or relax credit in Canada typically give rise to large inflows or outflows of capital taking advantage of the changed relative conditions in the domestic and foreign markets.[1] Under a fixed-rate system, a monetary authority seeking to raise interest rates by selling bonds

[1]R. E. Caves and G. L. Reuber, *Canadian Economic Policy and the Impact of International Capital Flows*, PPAC series "Canada in the Atlantic Economy," no. 10, Toronto, University of Toronto Press, 1969.

finds itself obliged to buy the foreign currency offered by foreign investors who wish to buy bonds at the now more attractive prices. The attempt then results in an exchange of foreign assets for domestic bonds in the monetary authority's portfolio rather than a change in the quantity of domestic money and the rate of interest. By and large, monetary policy in a country with a fixed exchange rate can control the volume of reserves, but it cannot cause movements of the rate of interest and the price level to differ very substantially from what is going on abroad.

The contemporary substantial unification of the economically advanced world's capital market renders monetary policy relatively ineffective in controlling prices and demand in the domestic economy. This leaves fiscal policy as the effective weapon. The shortcoming of this situation is that fiscal policy is on the whole a clumsy and inflexible instrument to use on a large scale for the control of the overall level of demand, especially in a federal state where various levels of government jockey for tax revenue and expenditure roles. Furthermore, fiscal policy has other goals than stabilization—redistributing income, supplying public goods and services, and guiding economic growth. This makes it difficult, if not undesirable, to put the whole weight of stabilization on fiscal policy. Conflicts may also arise between budget policies needed for growth and those needed for full employment. For instance, it might be desirable to develop a budgetary surplus in order to stimulate growth, because the private sector does not save enough over the long run owing to progressive income tax or some such reason, whereas for short-term-stabilization purposes a stimulus through a budgetary deficit would be necessary.

The difficulty in achieving balance of payments adjustment in the present international monetary system has led to the application of controls on trade and capital movements in an attempt to curb the manifestation of imbalances. Such controls by an important nation cause misallocation of resources for others, as well as for itself, and raise questions concerning the appropriate response from others. In periods of a generally cooperative atmosphere among advanced countries, the question has not been how to retaliate, but how to harmonize policies in order to minimize the distorting effect of other countries' controls. Harmonization has sometimes consisted of the spread of cooperative controls to other countries. The Canadian experience of the 1960s with U.S. controls is a case of cooperative response between two countries in which the U.S. government adjusted its control policies to take into account Canadian needs, while Canada in turn instituted controls that harmonized with those of the United States.

During the 1960s, the United States, concerned over its weakening balance of payments position, instituted a series of increasingly stringent measures restricting the outflow of capital and hastening the repatriation of earnings. The response of the Canadian government was to harmonize its policy on the export of capital to Europe with that of the United States so as to prevent the leakage of American capital to Europe through Canada. In exchange, the United States removed its controls from exports of capital to Canada.

The result of the accommodation of Canada within a system of U.S. financial controls and Canada's harmonization with American policy was to improve the condition of the Canadian economy, not only as compared to its position were it outside Washington's controls, but also with respect to its position if the U.S. balance of payments had been corrected by a more orthodox reliance on interest rates and fiscal policy. The reason for this is that the U.S. controls can be looked upon as an alternative to a tightening of monetary conditions in the United States, which would have raised the cost of imported capital to Canada. Such action would have reduced the amount imported and the rate of return for other factors cooperating with capital in Canada. To put it another way, the U.S. controls lowered the price of capital in the United States relative to its level in a non-discriminatory situation and relative to its level if the United States relied on monetary policy to correct its balance of payments position. The lower interest rates in the United States permitted Canada to borrow on more favourable terms and had a favourable effect on Canadian income.

The foregoing discussion indicates that the logic of the IMF system of fixed exchange rates obliges countries to engage in substantial macro-economic policy harmonization, even if sometimes haphazardly and in a decentralized manner, at the peril of the collapse of the international monetary system.

The United States plays a central role in a fixed-exchange-rate system because its economy produces half the total output of the world and generates half the world's money. Its money supply is dominated by considerations relating to domestic U.S. goals for employment and prices, and when it changes the level of its domestic rates of interest, it usually carries along those of the rest of the world. The U.S. dollar is the only existing currency qualified for a widespread reserve-currency role. The monetary policy of the United States has thus tended to have a dominant effect on the rate of world inflation via its effect on the price level of its vast currency area as transmitted through both world interest rates and the level of world reserves.

For Canada, the advantages of a fixed-rate system are chiefly the short-term certainty of the exchange-rate level and the consequent ease of calculating foreign prices, because the rate can change only rarely, even though sometimes substantially, rather than continuously by small amounts. The disadvantage is the loss of control over the domestic price level and the excessive dependence on fiscal policy to influence demand.

The question then arises whether this degree of integration and harmonization of policy is necessary to the efficient allocation of resources and the maintenance of full employment in Canada. The very clear answer is that it is not; on the contrary, the fixed-exchange-rate system is a handicap.

A flexible exchange rate permits divergence of price changes in Canada from those in the United States, because the two are related to each other through the now changing exchange rate. A flexible exchange rate restores the efficacy of monetary policy affecting demand, because flows of capital induced by attempts to change the relationship between Canadian and foreign interest rates no longer affect merely the level of foreign-exchange reserves but instead also affect the exchange rate and hence the relationship of exports to imports. For instance, a Canadian movement to relative monetary ease under a flexible-exchange-rate system, just as under a regime of fixed rates, results in only a small relative decrease in the level of Canadian interest rates, owing to the high elasticity of international supplies of capital. However, under a flexible-rate system the outflow of capital increases the demand for foreign currency and causes a depreciation of the Canadian dollar, resulting in an increase in exports relative to imports, which is an expansionary force.

Thus a flexible rate restores to Canadian authorities an instrument of economic control and the possibility of managing demand and the price level to achieve superior economic performance. The possibility of superior performance does not ensure actual superiority, but to reject a flexible-rate system is to reject the possibility of achieving this element of improved performance, and it ties Canadian policy to that of foreign countries. A self-confident government seeks to maximize its autonomy where its freedom of action does not conflict with the interests of other nations.

A flexible exchange rate for Canada does not interfere with the policies of the governments of other countries. Their macro-economic policies gain freedom from concern over the level of their foreign liabilities (Canadian foreign-exchange reserves). The flexible rate does not impede the efficient allocation of resources from the structural point of view because it leaves largely unchanged the pattern of relative prices within each country. On the contrary, the freedom from balance of payments constraints that the system provides relieves countries of the necessity or temptation to use exchange controls and so increases allocative efficiency in international trade and payments.

The conclusion reached by this analysis of the international harmonization of balance of payments policies is that the extent of harmonization varies with the type of exchange system in force, a fixed-rate system requiring more harmonization than a flexible-rate system. Harmonization of balance of payments policies among advanced countries is widespread, though imperfectly coordinated. Freer trade, regional or multilateral, would not in general provide a significantly increased need for policy harmonization of macro-economic balance of payments measures or for a different type of harmonization than is evolving in any event. Furthermore, with or without freer trade, the instituting of particular controls by the United States and even perhaps by countries less important in Canada's economic relations would require Canadian responses, the nature of which would depend on the particular circumstance.

### The harmonization of taxes and expenditure

The authors of the four important studies of tax and expenditure harmonization under conditions of freer or free trade prepared for the Atlantic Economic Studies Program[2] agree that an efficient tax system leaves the structure of prices of goods and services within each country as it would be in the absence of the tax. In other words, a tax system that treats all commodities and all activities alike leaves money prices proportional to the real costs of production and does not distort the allocation of resources from the basis of comparative advantage.[3]

In general, the conditions of efficiency are maintained if rates of domestic taxes are uniform on different activities within each country, even if rates differ from country to country. Furthermore, taxes can be levied either on consumption (this is the destination basis) or on production (the origin basis), and the principle applies to income taxes as well as to single-stage production or consumption taxes. It is possible to have taxes in one country levied on one basis and in another country on the other basis without distorting the conditions for efficiency. In fact, it is quite compatible with efficiency to have a system based partly on origin and partly on destination within one country, so long as the combination is applied uniformly to all activities. Hence, harmonization, or even coordination, of tax policies is

[2]H. G. Johnson, P. Wonnacott, H. Shibata, *Harmonization of National Economic Policies under Free Trade* (a three-part analysis), and H. Shibata, *Fiscal Harmonization under Free Trade: Principles and Their Applications to a Canada-U.S. Free Trade Area*, PPAC series "Canada in the Atlantic Economy," nos. 3 and 9, Toronto, University of Toronto Press, 1968, 1969.
[3]The relative money prices of goods net of taxes may not be proportional to their real cost because of unequal monopoly power or some other distortion. Taxation could be used to restore this proportionality. Because this source of inefficiency is distinct from the general tax and expenditure problem, it is dealt with elsewhere.

not logically essential to efficiency in international commerce, with or without free trade.

In regard to welfare under conditions of *balanced* trade, there is also equivalence of effect from either the origin or the destination basis, although this is not an obvious point. A domestic consumer will pay the same prices for domestically produced goods, whichever of these two bases of taxation is in force at home. Thus, the different bases of taxation will affect his decision only with respect to goods produced abroad. If taxation is on a destination basis, he pays taxes on imported goods that are equal to the taxes that he pays on goods produced at home.[4] If taxation is on the basis of origin, he pays no taxes on imported goods. Meanwhile, the foreign purchaser of goods produced in the first country pays no taxes on imports if the first country's taxation is based on destination; but if that country's taxation is on the basis of origin, then the foreign purchaser pays taxes to the first country's government on such imports.

Now the crucial point is that the value of imports and exports must be balanced for long-run international equilibrium. Suppose, for example, that imports appear to become particularly attractive from the tax point of view because a change in the taxation basis of the first country from destination to origin means that these imports are no longer taxed. This tends to raise demand for imports in the first country, for they are now cheaper, and to depress foreign demand for the first country's exports because they are now taxed at origin. Thus, the first country will have an excess of imports over exports. The result is to bid up the price of the foreign country's currency so that the prices of foreign goods in the first country rise—or, if the exchange rate is fixed, to raise the price level directly in the foreign market and to lower it at home. The equilibrium is found again where the value of exports and imports is equal. That equilibrium is at a different exchange rate or relative price level for each tax situation, but the volume of trade is the same. In the long run, at equilibrium, the basis of taxation, whether destination or origin, does not affect the volume of trade nor the combination of goods chosen by consumers in the two countries.

The revenues of the two governments are unaltered by the change in the basis of taxation described above. We assume for simplicity that the revenues of the foreign government are zero. The domestic government receives the same amount of tax using the origin or the destination basis—provided that the rates of tax are the same. Using the destination basis, the government

---

[4]Whether or not taxes are paid by the foreign producer to foreign governments is irrelevant, because they would be levied or not under either tax system in the home country; but we will, for simplicity, assume that there is no taxation of any sort in foreign countries.

receives tax revenue on all that the domestic consumer purchases—namely, domestic production for domestic consumption plus consumption of imports. On the origin basis, the government receives tax revenue from domestic production for domestic consumption plus export sales. So long as exports and imports are equal in value, the total tax revenue in the two cases must be the same.

Although the general principle is correct that the effects of taxation on the basis of destination and of origin (and this includes income tax) are equivalent and that, hence, the bases of taxation need not be harmonized internationally, it is possible to choose between them according to criteria that may have relevance in particular cases. One case is that of transition from one basis of taxation to the other. It is evident that a change to origin from destination must be more difficult politically than a move in the other direction, because it implies an increase in demand for foreign goods that have become free of tax and therefore cheaper at the initial exchange rate. The country switching to the origin principle then suffers a deficit in its balance of payments and must adjust in a way that may be painful.

A purely political consideration is the appearance of an advantage of destination taxes to the general public, which sees that on the destination basis imports are taxed, whereas under the origin principle imports are not taxed but domestic production for domestic consumption is. This is an illusory advantage in the long run, as has been seen, because both taxes maintain the same relative prices of goods produced in the two countries and the same tax payments to government, assuming balance of payments equilibrium. Thus, the only economic legitimacy to this point is that a change from a destination to an origin basis is deflationary, whereas a change from an origin to a destination basis increases demand for a country's exports and is therefore inflationary.

An advantage of the origin principle is that it eliminates the need for customs administration between countries that have no tariffs. If all countries in the world applied taxation on the origin basis and had no tariffs, customs administration could be done away with, because all taxation would be applied where goods were produced. This point is unaffected by differences in the rates of taxes at origin. This advantage of origin taxation would also apply, of course, within a customs union having a common external tariff. In this case, goods from abroad would all pay the same tariff, wherever imported, and goods within the common market would not be subject to taxes at the border because they would be taxed at origin. However, a free trade area with different national external tariffs needs to maintain control on intra-area trade, in order to control re-exports. That is to say, something has to be done about goods from outside the area that may come in through the country with the lowest tariff on the relevant product and be re-exported to countries within the area having higher external tariffs on that product. Hence, for a free trade area the origin basis cuts down administration at the border only as it applies to goods produced within the area. The advantage of the origin basis is less pronounced in this case than for a customs union.

Income taxes are a kind of origin tax, and the general principle applies with respect to them also—that is, that differences in tax rates between countries do not distort the efficient allocation of resources so long as, within each country, the tax rates are applied equally to all sources of income. This neutrality of income tax applies even if the tax is progressive. Different rates of income tax in the two countries do bring about distortions, however, if all sources of income are not taxed. In such a case, factors of production in the country with higher rates of tax tend to shift into those occupations in which part of the income is not taxed.

This discussion has shown that efficiency in production and in international exchange does not require harmonization of tax rates or of types, except that within each country taxes should be equally applied on all activities. However, two exceptions should be noted. One arises if the social value of a certain commodity differs from its factor cost; this consideration may require differences in tax rates between commodities. The other arises if factors of production migrate from one country to the other; that problem may necessitate the coordination or harmonization of tax and expenditure policy.

The rule of equal taxes on all activities is based on the assumption that the value of the output of each commodity or service to society is equal to its cost of production, which is the value of the services of the factors that are used in producing the commodity in question. This is the general case, but exceptions are widely felt to exist, and governments consequently attempt to bring about greater equality between social and private returns by taxing those activities where the social return falls below the private return. Alternatively, governments could subsidize those industries that are too small because the private returns are less than the social returns. For instance, motor vehicles may cause social costs through congestion and pollution that are greater than the private costs paid by their operators. The returns to the individual operating a vehicle exceed the contribution to social welfare from its operation. In such a case, the efficient allocation of resources requires restraining automobile operations, and this can be achieved by applying a higher-than-normal rate of tax on that activity. One could add many familiar examples of higher taxes on activities from which the social returns are said to be relatively low, such as tobacco and alcohol production. Such differences in tax rates, if properly applied, represent a social philosophy; they need not distort the allocation of resources nor the course of international trade.

It must be recognized that high taxes are sometimes levied on particular products for reasons not of social philosophy but of fiscal expediency arising because taxes are easily collected on a commodity for which demand is inelastic. High rates of taxation may also be applied for the purpose of indirect protection of domestic activity. This might occur where high taxes are applied to an imported commodity that is a close substitute for a domestically produced commodity.

The existence of these three possible reasons for exceptionally high taxes on particular commodities or processes, only one of which is legitimate for efficiency, requires that governments be explicit as to the reasons for particularly high rates and, preferably, that such exceptional rates be harmonized between members of a free trade area or a customs union—or, indeed, between all countries that have especially close economic relations.

The other force that tends to require harmonization of tax rates, and to some extent of expenditure policy, is the mobility of factors of production between advanced countries. Capital and labour move between countries in response to differences in the real income that they receive in different locations. This is, in turn, affected by the taxes that the owners have to pay and by the services that are provided to them by the governments of different countries.

Taxes are raised to provide the governmental services that people want. The difficulty is that services consumed by a particular individual are not necessarily equal in value to the taxes that that individual pays. Any given structure of taxes and provision of governmental services gives greater net benefits to some individuals than to others. Consequently, if the structure of taxes and benefits is not harmonized between countries, some inducement exists for individuals to move. Even if an individual receives services equivalent in cost to the taxes he pays, he may still be inclined to emigrate because he considers such services less useful to him personally than other things he could afford with the tax money saved if he lived abroad. In general, the difference between what an individual pays in taxes and receives in governmental services varies with his income, his ownership of resources, the industry in which he uses his resources, and the region in which he lives. Such considerations relate to one of the important purposes of taxation and the provision of public goods—to redistribute income so as to favour or disfavour particular industries or regions. By and large, these factors mean that the more wealthy the individual, the less likely is he to receive the full benefit of his tax payments from governmental services, and the more likely is he to be attracted by areas of low taxes.

Corporations benefit directly from relatively few governmental welfare measures, and, in any event, the owners of a corporation may benefit from welfare measures in countries other than their firm's base. Consequently, corporations respond to tax differences more than to differences in governmental expenditures. The importance of income tax rates on corporations, coupled with the mobility of such corporations, results in the virtual harmonization of corporate income tax rates between countries—notably Canada and the United States—and the harmonization of business taxes, including provincial and state taxes, between other jurisdictions. In addition to corporations, wealthy individuals whose income is derived, in larger proportion than for other income groups, from capital are also particularly sensitive to individual tax rates, and they too have the best information and a relatively greater ability to move. Thus, the concentration of capital in the hands of corporations and of wealthy individuals means that the mobility of capital is high, as compared with that of other factors of production, and also that movements of capital are more in response to tax differences than to differences in expenditure policies between governments.

The more interdependent national economies become—as they might through the creation of free trade areas or customs unions—the greater the usefulness of uniformity in the net treatment of individuals through taxes and expenditures. The closer the relationship between different economic areas, the more important does harmonization appear as the most direct way of treating individuals equally in different areas so as not to distort the allocation of resources within this larger economy, be it that of the world or of a region.

In summary, then, it has been shown that the harmonization of tax and expenditure patterns is not necessary between countries for the efficient allocation of resources and for international trade based on comparative advantage. However, the high degree of mobility of labour and, especially, of capital in the modern world makes it difficult to maintain widely varying tax rates on factors. The country with unusually high taxes finds that it is subject to an outward migration of factors and is ultimately induced to conform to the common level. Discriminatorily high taxes on certain activities must be justified clearly on social grounds as a measure to equalize social and private costs or returns. Otherwise, such taxation appears to be guided merely by fiscal expediency and to distort the efficient allocation of resources and the pattern of trade based on comparative advantage, which invites international retaliation or other difficulties.

*The harmonization of competition, transportation, and developmental policies*

International trade brings gains to a country even if the production of the countries with which it trades is distorted by inefficiencies and the misallocation of resources. The maximization of income for a single country through international trade consists of comparing the relative prices at which foreign countries supply goods and services of various sorts with the relative costs of producing such goods and services at home. The country imports foreign goods that are comparatively low in price in exchange for goods and services produced relatively cheaply at home. Thus, gains from trade arise whether or not the supply prices of the foreign countries reveal the relative real costs of production of the various goods and services in these countries. However, since domestic imports and exports are guided by prices, it is a condition of efficiency that domestic prices should reveal the real costs of production at home. Otherwise, divergencies between relative prices and relative real costs of production at home could cause a country to export goods that, despite their low prices, were in fact relatively expensive to produce, and to import things that might actually be better produced at home.

The importance, both domestically and internationally, of having relative prices that accurately reflect domestic real costs of efficient production is the principal reason why many countries have followed policies designed to maintain competition in the domestic economy. Selective tax or subsidy policies have also been used where prices did not reflect real costs, as seen by government, because of external costs or benefits not borne by the producer or consumer of the commodity.

Foreign supply prices may be artificial, in the sense of not reflecting relative real costs of production abroad, either because the foreign exporters restrict supply in order to obtain a monopoly profit from the sale of their commodities in other countries or because foreign prices are lowered through an artificial mechanism—perhaps a subsidy on the part of the foreign government. If the home country lacks sufficient economic or political power to affect these practices or policies of foreign countries, it may nevertheless gain (as already noted) from engaging in international trade on the basis of the foreign supply prices even if they do not reflect real costs. Where the home country does have an influence on foreign prices, either by economic bargaining or by diplomacy, then it should obviously seek to alter the high prices of its imports resulting from monopolistic behaviour in the other country. It should not, however, discourage foreign subsidies on the goods it imports, because such measures lower the landed price of its purchases from abroad —clearly a gain for the consumer and the balance of payments. On the other hand, a foreign subsidy on goods competing with the home country's export goods reduces the volume of trade by decreasing the market abroad—a loss which that country would wish to prevent.

These general principles apply to the home country's international trade whether it is carried on subject to tariffs or in a free trade area. Nevertheless, it must be recognized that a country entering formally into a free trade arrangement is supported by a public that presumably approves of an open international economy, but only if there are satisfactory guarantees of "fair" competition. As a practical matter, this requirement involves some harmonization of competitive conditions and policies. Partly, this sentiment is similar to the point of view that some uniformity of taxation is called for, on either an origin or a destination basis, where there is close cooperation in a trading area, even though such steps are not logically necessary, as we have noted, to achieve gains from trade. But, also, the sentiment is founded on the principle that the purpose of free trade—including a formal free trade area—is to increase the efficiency of production in the area as a whole. This objective will be achieved, and the arrangement will last, only if the relatively inefficient industries in each country give way to the relatively efficient industries in the others, thus increasing the volume of international trade. Gains arise in the entire community from this process through specialization in the production of relatively efficient industries, and perhaps dynamic gains can also be obtained from this process of rationalization as the relatively efficient industries in each country expand and take advantage of economies of large-scale production, where such exist.

The necessity to seek a price system that is neutral in its guidance of trade between partner countries, in the sense that it does not distort relative prices from relative real costs of production, implies that certain policies that countries might initiate or tolerate in other circumstances would have to be either eliminated or harmonized. One such example is the application of prohibitions to restraints of trade on exports to partner countries. Both the Webb-Pomerene Act in the United States and anti-combines legislation in Canada exempt from anti-combines prosecution any economic activities that are exclusively directed to exports. This arrangement allows the exploitation of foreign buyers in a way that would not be permitted at home. Clearly, the formation of a free trade area would require the abolition of such an anomaly to equalize conditions of competition within the area.

Restrictive behaviour and collusive practices also affect imports, since they are designed either to protect inefficient producers or to create excess profits for strong efficient firms that dominate markets. A change in the size of the market as a result of tariff elimination would to some extent break down restrictive behaviour and force more efficient production. This is so because more entities, each with less impact on price than previously, would face each other and compete for a share of the larger market. Similarly, the strong firms that were already producing efficiently would now be faced with a large number of competitors and would be less able to maintain a monopoly level of profits. But even with tariffs, an important goal of restrictive business practices is to moderate the effect of imports on competition and prices at home, either by putting pressure on domestic buyers not to purchase foreign goods or by collusive arrangements with the foreign suppliers of imported goods. The inducement to strengthen this aspect of business behaviour might be increased, under free trade, because other means of maintaining existing patterns of production and prices would be reduced with the elimination of barriers to trade.

Policies would need to respond to such a strengthening of domestic restrictive practices and to international cartelization. This could be done through the coordination of anti-combines policies by the governments of the various countries, employing the instruments of national policy to attack particular instances of restrictive business practices that interfered with the normal course of trade and production. Alternatively, governments of the partner countries could engage in a genuine harmonization of anti-combines policies which would consist of treating all trade with partner countries under the same rules as are applied to internal trade. The process of harmonization might proceed to the point at which the entire area was regarded by each government as the field of application for national anti-combines policy and the policies applied by all governments were the same.

As a quantitative and practical matter, it is very difficult to judge the significance that restrictive practices would have in distorting the pattern of prices and the course of trade in a free trade area. In neither the EEC nor EFTA has the problem acquired much importance, despite the initial concern of the EEC Commission with monopolistic practices. It may thus be that any free trade area that Canada joined, thus expanding manyfold the size of market open to Canadian producers, would of itself so increase competitive pressures as to make restrictive practices much less effective than they are now—and, indeed, to render them inoperative for all practical purposes.

Governments may not only support or restrict the policies and practices of private business that can cause divergence of relative prices from relative real costs; they may themselves engage in policies having similar effects. All governments have as an important objective the support of business within their jurisdictions or the development of particular industries or regions. Two widely employed policies to these ends are discriminatory purchasing practices, used by both national and local governments (and provincial or state governments in federal countries), and devices such as favourable taxation and the provision of subsidies and other aids to assist particular industries or regions.

Governments typically give a margin of preference to local producers when purchasing goods and services.[5] This practice arouses relatively little intergovernmental protest, partly because it is so universally practised and partly because it is to a substantial extent unseen, the margin of preference and the existence of the preference itself being typically unpublicized. Where the preference is statutory, as in the "Buy America Act" governing purchases by federal government agencies in the United States, the rule attracts a great deal of comment. It could be expected that in a free trade area such policies would require at least a substantial degree of harmonization, so that the margins of preference would be the same everywhere; preferably, however, governments would agree to abolish all these arrangements. In the case of Canada, the elimination of preferential purchasing at the federal level could easily be envisaged as a consequence of international agreement, but the independence of lower-level governments would make it difficult to remove such practices in provincial and local purchasing.

It was shown in an earlier section of this chapter that a tax rate can legitimately be varied among activities so as to equalize differences between social and private costs in some of them. In the same way, variations in tax rates or in spending can be used discriminatingly among activities for other general social purposes, such as favouring a particular region in order to stimulate its growth or to guard against its decline. Such developmental policy consists of increasing the positive difference between benefits received and taxes paid by individuals and industries within the region. In Canada, such discriminatory tax and expenditure treatment is especially noted in the arrangements governing the mining and oil industries, on the one hand, and in special assistance to the Atlantic provinces, on the other. As with other cases in which particular activities are favoured by tax and expenditure policies, justification for such special treatment must be made clear in order to avoid arousing suspicion in trading partners as the economic relations among nations become closer and their interdependence increases. Unless fears of unfair competition are allayed, retaliation may arise, and the attempt to rationalize the international allocation of resources through trade may break down.

Canada's position is unusual in this regard because many of the firms benefiting from the particularly favourable treatment of mining and oil companies, as well as some of the companies enjoying special consideration

[5]Albert Breton, *Discriminatory Government Policies in Federal Countries*, Montreal, Canadian Trade Committee, 1967.

in the "slow-growth" regions of the country, are owned abroad, so that their profits accrue chiefly to foreigners. Thus, whereas the interests of industries in the United States are sometimes affected adversely by the discriminatory results of favourable treatment afforded certain industries and regions in Canada, part of the benefit of these policies goes to residents of foreign countries, especially the United States. The benefits consist either of higher profits for operations in Canada or of lower export prices. (And if export prices in industries supplying raw materials to the foreign parent company are lower than would otherwise be the case, this tends to augment the profits of the foreign firm.) In either event, the special treatment of these industries leads to greater expansion in Canada than would occur if no discriminatorily favourable treatment had been given, and it thus constitutes a transfer from the Canadian taxpayer, who receives no favours and has to pay more taxes to maintain government revenue, to the foreign firm producing in Canada (or using Canadian products abroad) or to the foreign consumer.

Subsidies of various sorts to aid the development of specific industries or particular regions within a country have also attracted international attention, especially where the impact of the policy on trade has been obvious. This occurs where the industry being aided is one whose products enter trade because expansion either improves its position to export or decreases the domestic share of the market going to imports. A less distorting type of development policy is that which is directed at providing services and infrastructure to a particular region, thus enabling it to attract capital for industries of all types. Insofar as such development leads to the attraction of industries with no particular role in international trade, the policy need not give rise to international tension or to pressure for harmonization. However, it is often the case that a region is suited best to a particular industry; if that industry is important in international trade, then problems arise similar to those in a situation of direct support to a trading industry.

The fact that development policies affect the pattern of trade does not make them unacceptable. They are widely accepted nationally, and provision is made for them within the European Economic Community. Thus, the instituting of freer trade would not lead to the abolishment of development policies. However, because they have effects similar to tariffs in some cases and to trade-promotion practices in others, their nature would have to be understood and their form negotiated, and limits would have to be placed on their extent through international harmonization or at least coordination. It is difficult to foresee whether, in the Canadian case, a free trade area would cause an increase or a decrease in the resources put into regional and industrial development policy. On the one hand, the necessity to negotiate —or, in any event, explain—the need for such support to lagging regions and industries would tend to reduce the extent of such support. The negotiators from other countries are likely to be less susceptible to the needs of particular regions or industries in Canada than are Canadian regional representatives. On the other hand, the experience of the EEC is that free trade strengthens the already flourishing industries in the partner countries so that the political pressures for support to the lagging industries and regions become stronger. Such an evolution might also take place in a free trade area of which Canada was a member, so that the pressure to ease the lot of declining industries would grow.

Transportation policies and practices[6] may, in a way very similar to tariffs, distort the pattern of trade. Tariffs are analogous to a transportation cost, being a tax on transporting commodities across an international border. Similarly, freight rates that are not based entirely on the costs of transportation also erect an artificial barrier or give an artificial subsidy to commodities going from one place to the other. Insofar as these discrepancies between freight rates and costs are discriminatory between international and national trade, their qualitative effect is identical to that of tariffs.

Freight rates do, however, tend to depart from the perfectly competitive pattern in which rates and costs would be proportional. This is so for two reasons. First, transportation firms, be they publicly or privately owned, tend to discriminate between regions and types of traffic in response to the competition to which they are subjected from other carriers. Thus, in areas and for commodities for which there are many alternative modes of transportation or routes, freight rates tend to be low, whereas in areas in which there is little competition a carrier will tend to raise rates as much as the markets will bear so as to increase its overall rate of return. Secondly, freight rates often do not correspond to relative costs, because regulatory authorities have a national bias which tends to raise rates on international transportation relative to those on entirely national routes. The typical policy applied to railway rates in Canada and the United States, as well as in other countries, is to treat international traffic as if it originated at the border. This practice has the effect of raising freight costs on international routes because it ignores the principle that freight rates decline with distance—the per-mile cost of transportation declines as the journey grows longer. Since international traffic is treated as the sum of two shorter routes rather than as one long route, the freight rates applied are increased as compared to national traffic. Another major feature of Canadian transportation policy is that specially arranged low transcontinental rates—"agreed charges"—are ap-

[6]John M. Munro, *Trade Liberalization and Transportation in International Trade*, PPAC series "Canada in the Atlantic Economy," no. 8, Toronto, University of Toronto Press, 1969.

plicable to particular types of traffic under specific conditions, which include the agreement by the shipper to send all his product by rail.

It is not possible at present to make a quantitative estimate of the distortion of freight rates compared with the pattern that would be dictated by relative costs, or to gauge the effect of this distortion on traffic. The effect in Canada varies with the commodity being transported and with the route. Obviously, the levels of freight rates, including any distortions in them, are likely to influence the routes followed by commodities to an extent proportional to the size and weight of the items involved, the relative distances of shipment, and the unit rate applicable. These factors are reflected statistically in the ratio of transportation costs to delivered prices. The higher this ratio, the greater is going to be the sensitivity of traffic to transport costs and the greater the distorting effect on the pattern of trade from divergences between rates and costs. The information available suggests that the ratio of freight costs to delivered prices of internationally traded commodities is extremely variable, ranging from nearly 25 percent on imports of fruits and vegetables into Canada to less than 5 percent for most manufactured commodities. Similarly, the ratio for exports of heavy and low-valued commodities (for example, chemical fertilizers and lumber and plywood) is high, whereas for manufactured commodities it tends to be much lower.

It is likely, therefore, that the degree of protection to national producers of manufactured products offered by the fact that international transportation rates are higher than national rates is relatively slight. Supposing the ratio of freight costs to delivered prices were around 5 percent, then the distorting element would be departures from this average—the probability is that these departures are somewhat larger on international trade and somewhat smaller on national production. This discrimination, which could not be more than a very few percentage points, would obviously have a much smaller effect than that of present tariff rates on manufactured products, which tend to average about 15 percent. On the other hand, for bulky commodities, where the ratio is typically much higher and where, in addition, the tariff barriers are usually very low or zero, the distorting effect of discriminatory freight rates becomes relatively more important as an instrument for affording protection to domestic sources of supply.

The discussion so far has been applied chiefly to *rail* transportation, because that is where the regulatory authorities have the greatest influence and where freight rates have been the most stable. Competition in the trucking industry tends to equalize the freight rates charged by various carriers and over different routes, so that within a country freight rates generally reflect the actual costs of transportation. However, the cost of transporting by truck across international borders is enlarged, as compared to the cost of domestic trucking, by the various regulations that are applied to international road-freight services. Thus a trucker transporting goods over a national boundary is faced with extra costs or absolute barriers. The former might include the unnecessary interchanging of trailers at the border, restrictions on the length of time a truck or trailer can remain abroad, and limitations as to the cargoes that may be carried in foreign countries. Absolute barriers would include the difficulty or impossibility of obtaining licences for trucking in another country. (However, it should be noted that lesser but similar difficulties are placed in the way of truckers in interprovincial traffic in Canada and interstate traffic in the United States.)

Traffic moving by ship is also subject to restrictions. Coastal traffic in Canada on the Pacific and Atlantic coasts can be carried only by ships registered in the British Commonwealth, while Canadian coastal traffic in the Great Lakes is limited to shipping registered in Canada. Thus, in the Great Lakes, Canadian coastal shipping is exclusively in the hands of Canadian ships for which the ceiling rates on commodities transported on the Great Lakes, but eventually to be exported, are limited to the extra costs that international seagoing ships incur when they extend their voyages to call for the bulk cargoes at Lake ports. Canadian coastal rates on the Pacific and Atlantic coasts tend to be kept down to international competitive standards by the eligibility of all British ships for traffic. The international trade from Canadian ports is open to competition from ships of all registry, and rates tend to be lower than the Canadian coastal rates. Thus, in shipping, the opposite situation to that of rail and truck transportation obtains. National shipping rates exceed international rates and hence, insofar as they are influential, amount to a tax on domestic transportation.

If Canada entered a free trade area with the United States, the structure of freight rates on international traffic would be subject to various influences that would tend to offset each other. The distorting effect of the present railway-freight policies and practices, which favour national as against international traffic, would tend to increase because the removal of tariffs would shift the pattern of trade more in a north-south direction and would then subject trade to higher freight costs per mile. On the other hand, the distances over which freight would be likely to travel would be less, since the distances between shipping points would generally not be as great in transborder trade as they are in east-west trade in Canada; therefore the freight cost per dollar's worth of merchandise would tend to fall and so would the distorting effect of discriminatory freight rates. Furthermore, the shorter north-south routes are more subject to truck competition, a factor that would tend to keep rates down to the lowest cost permitted by the penalties that administrative obstacles place upon trucking across international borders.

The efficient allocation of resources in a free trade area would not require the international harmonization of transportation policies, in view of the relatively slight distorting effect that such policies appear to have on trade in manufactured goods at present. Nevertheless, any movement tending to bring governmental regulations into conformity would be an improvement, especially if railway-freight regulation moved in the direction of present Canadian policy, which is to allow the carriers to price competitively. It is evident that the movement towards harmonization would be exceedingly difficult because of the multitude of local interests affected in the United States and because trucking regulations are in significant measure in the hands of provincial and state authorities.

### The harmonization of non-tariff barriers to trade

Non-tariff barriers have traditionally been defined as all those laws, regulations, and administrative procedures that impose costs on international trade that are additional to the tariff. It is now necessary to add to this definition those hidden or explicit subsidies that affect international trade. These are not barriers to trade in the proper sense, but they are included in this category because they distort the course of trade from the pattern established by comparative advantage, thereby creating inefficiencies and often giving rise to destructive retaliatory responses.

It is evident that some non-tariff trade barriers are inevitable, simply because all forms of governmental intervention imply procedural burdens. Thus, even in a free trade area, the necessity to maintain customs barriers between partner countries to prevent re-exports from one to the other implies the control of interpartner trade and, therefore, a greater cost for this than for purely domestic trade.

Devising coordinated or harmonized policies to deal with non-tariff barriers is particularly important today. Tariffs among industrial countries are at historically low levels, and it is crucial to prevent the substituting of largely invisible protection for the visible tariff. The visible tariff is now under control and unlikely to rise again unless there is a breakdown in the solidarity of industrial countries. In the past, procedural barriers have varied in importance, as has the tariff, with changes in desire for protection that have been largely induced by variations in business conditions. Now that the tariff cannot readily be changed, the inducement for altering invisible barriers is all the greater.

An examination of recent Canadian history illustrates the variability of invisible barriers. During the depression of the 1930s, Canada engaged very widely in the use of official valuation for imports, a practice that typically resulted in values of imports for duty purposes exceeding their invoice values. These artificially high values gave rise to high rates of duty, but they also led to the application of dumping duties equal to the difference between the invoice price and the official valuation. Canada's important international position right after the Second World War, the strength of its export interests, and Ottawa's support for the General Agreement on Tariffs and Trade led to a complete reform in Canadian valuation practices, so that imports were valued, with very few exceptions, at the prices at which they were in fact bought. However, economic problems gave rise to some departures from this non-discriminatory practice, and in the early 1950s there was a return to administrative valuation in a few instances of "particularly sensitive" imports. The practice spread, and in 1970, with a period of business slowdown, Canada resorted to establishing artificially high minimum import prices for shirts from certain underdeveloped countries. This type of increase in administrative protection should be subjected to at least a standstill, lest it lead to a competitive round of international trade restrictions. A second, more ambitious goal for action would be to develop a program that would reduce invisible barriers to the inescapable minimum. The justification for such steps would be the principle that protection should be explicit in the tariff and not hidden in administrative and other procedures.

There is widespread fear today that non-tariff barriers will grow so as to negate the gains from reduced tariffs achieved in the Kennedy Round and before. The GATT has had the matter under surveillance for the past few years but has been unable to obtain an agreement from member countries to apply a standstill to non-tariff practices. The activities of the GATT Secretariat have been largely devoted to compiling a classified list of non-tariff barriers and practices, with an intention to launch future large-scale negotiations attempting to control non-tariff barriers. With recent pressure from the United States because of its balance of payments difficulties, Japan and the EEC have agreed to begin these negotiations in 1973, and Canada has expressed its full support for such an undertaking.

Some non-tariff barriers could be eliminated by multilateral agreement; others could be harmonized; in yet other cases, where these practices reflect genuine social needs and goals, it is probable that individual national practices of this kind must be allowed to remain.

Traditional non-tariff barriers have included the imposition of quotas on imports, artificial dumping duties, outright subsidies, and import surcharges. These are blatant instruments of protection that are used less frequently today than in the past by industrialized countries, except for occasional balance of payments purposes, and they might be made subject to an international agreement to forgo their use. Other important non-tariff barriers include uncertain, costly, and lengthy customs procedures for valuation or classification of imports, complicated marking regulations, unnecessary health, safety, and technological standards, and, very important for many countries, discriminatory purchasing by public agencies favouring domestic sources.

Newer varieties of non-tariff obstacles are the so-called "voluntary" export restraints which certain importing countries have induced other, often less developed, countries to place on the volume of their shipments of highly competitive goods.[7] These restraints are voluntary in no real sense and have flourished because the exporting governments believed such barriers would be less permanent than the alternative old-fashioned quotas on the part of the importing countries. There is indication that the Japanese government, at any rate, may be changing its mind. Governments also stimulate exports competitively by giving loans to exporters at uneconomically low rates of interest and by extending insurance to export trade at rates that do not cover costs.

A competitive international economic environment in which comparative costs determine the course of trade requires the abolition of quota restrictions on imports. The version of these devices that industrialized countries, including Canada, have persuaded exporting nations such as Japan and many underdeveloped countries to impose on their exports of textiles, shoes, steel and steel products, and electric equipment should also be eliminated. The same is true of arrangements that set minimum prices for imports, usually of textiles, for protective purposes so that the domestic consumer cannot get benefit from the low costs of production abroad. The question of public purchasing at discriminatory prices has already been discussed in the section on competition policy. However, a related aspect of this problem is the practice in some countries of public purchasing from domestic suppliers at high prices on condition that these firms sell more abroad. Such a policy amounts to an export subsidy which rules of fair international competition would abolish. Other export subsidies that flourish in the field of agriculture and shipbuilding should also be subject to restraint through international negotiations.

Easy credit to exporting industries and credit insurance at artificially low rates are forms of export subsidy that ought also to be controlled by rules developed in international negotiations. The practice of governmental financing could not be removed, but it could be made susceptible to certain rules, such as a minimum limit to interest rates at a level equal to or greater than the rate paid on its own borrowings by the government giving credit.

[7]Caroline Pestieau and Jacques Henry, *Non-Tariff Barriers as a Problem in International Development*, Montreal, Canadian Economic Policy Committee, 1972.

Insurance schemes might be limited by the requirement that their operations cover their costs. It should be noted that the granting of low-interest-rate export credit and of artificially cheap export insurance is today a special benefit to importers in underdeveloped countries and in Eastern Europe. Insofar as such competition amounts to a deliberate development aid, it might be replaced by explicit international grants or loans.

Many administrative barriers should be subjected relatively easily to international regulation. Requirements that imported goods should show marks of origin can be justified on the grounds that such marking provides information to the purchaser. It is doubtless the case that labeling is just as often an advantage for the sale of goods (as, for example, in women's clothing made in France) as it is a disadvantage. However, some regulations require marking that disfigures goods or is unreasonably costly and could fairly easily be made equitable and non-restrictive through international harmonization.

Progress should also be feasible in the harmonization of technical standards. A tendency exists for importing countries to protect domestic producers by requiring technical standards that differ from those of the potential exporter. Such an invisible barrier to trade clearly reduces the efficiency of worldwide production by fostering high-cost local production, reducing the interchangeability of parts, and limiting economies of scale that might grow with international specialization within the industries affected. Some progress has been made in Europe in the adoption of common technical standards for electronic components, a development that is currently being severely attacked by the United States as a protective device. The lesson to be drawn from this experience is that technical standardization should take place in international commissions with universal membership, so that the suspicion of protectionist motives could be dispelled and obvious gains achieved for industrial efficiency and consumer benefit. Nevertheless, it should be observed that the cost of bringing equipment to common standards would be high, so that rapid progress in international harmonization in this field is not to be expected.

The case for the harmonization of health and safety standards is less justifiable, because the views and requirements of different countries with respect to the minimum quality of commodities sold in the domestic market may legitimately differ. Quality is related to cost, and countries with low standards of living may with reason approve of commodities that have lower minimum quality than is acceptable in other countries. The appropriate procedure for health and safety standards consists of applying the same requirements for imported as for domestic production.[8]

[8]Some grey areas exist in the construction of any general rule. For instance, the

In the years ahead, increasing attention is likely to be given to the establishment of anti-pollution standards, and the effects of this development will be felt in regulations governing the specifications of imported products (for example, automobiles), as well as in the production of commodities that enter into international trade. Avoiding protection disguised as anti-pollution measures is not a difficult problem in theory, because the divergence between private and social cost can be handled by appropriate commodity taxation. If the excess of social cost over the cost borne by the private individual arises from the use of the merchandise (as, for instance, in the pollution caused by automobiles), then the commodity should be taxed on the basis of destination so that the cost of both the domestic and the imported merchandise is brought up to the social level. If, on the other hand, it is the production of the commodity that is socially costly, as might be the case of river pollution from pulp production, then the taxation ought to be on the origin basis so that both domestic and foreign consumers would pay the full cost of the merchandise they use.

Elaborate systems of classification of imports and artificial systems for their valuation give rise to delays and uncertainty which are themselves also barriers to trade. The nature of any appeal process from the decision of customs officials may also introduce varying degrees of complexity, uncertainty, or delay. The harmonization of systems of classification for imports does not necessarily bring about a simplification of the system, although it moves in the direction of efficiency by abolishing national peculiarities. Today European countries classify according to the Brussels Tariff Nomenclature, which is much simpler than the complex systems used by Canada and the United States. Adoption of the Brussels Nomenclature by these two countries would bring a gain of both sorts, standardization and simplification.

The aim for valuation should be international harmonization around the principle that value for duty purposes is the price actually paid by the importer, exception being made only for cases of predatory dumping in which there is sufficient evidence of injury, as under the present satisfactory GATT rules. The problem of harmonizing valuation between countries in which there are import tariffs is obviously pressing, since any fall in tariff rates can be compensated by artificially high values for duty purposes. European countries and some others apply the Brussels definition of value, which uses the invoice as the main basis for calculating value for duty. The adoption of this definition by other nations, such as the United States, Canada, and

---

requirement for electric ranges in Canada that each element should be separately fused, whereas ranges in the United States may be centrally fused, is conceivably a necessary safety feature for consumers. However, it is suspected by potential U.S. exporters of being an artificial barrier to trade.

Japan, would be a major move towards harmonization on a simpler basis. It would also involve the removal of the most flagrant artificiality in valuation practised anywhere—the "American Selling Price" system affecting U.S. imports of benzoid chemicals and pharmaceuticals as well as some other products. This device, which covers about one percent of total U.S. imports, establishes values for duty on the basis of the domestic manufacturers' list price, rather than on the price actually charged by the foreign exporter. Rates of duty exceeding 100 percent are frequently calculated by this mechanism.

This discussion of non-tariff barriers indicates that substantial gains in international efficiency could be made through the elimination of certain non-tariff barriers and the harmonization of other national practices that affect trade. Such gains would occur whether or not free trade was instituted. Harmonization of many trade-restrictive measures, such as complex technical standards or health and safety requirements, is most easily achieved among countries with similar levels of industrialization and standards of living. These include some of the very countries likely to establish free trade areas, so that harmonization may well proceed hand in hand with those types of regional arrangements in which, in any event, problems of classification and valuation would disappear, since no duty would be applied to inter-partner trade.

*Transitional policies*

Any major change in governmental policy has economic implications for firms, labour, and other owners of factors of production, some of whom benefit while others lose. Such adjustments in the positions of individuals and firms are likely to be particularly great in a movement to regional or world free trade, which would involve both the removal of tariff protection from industry and the elimination or harmonization of non-tariff barriers to trade. The removal of import tariffs in foreign countries would be of obvious benefit to many Canadian producers. The clearest gainers would be those already selling abroad, whose goods either would yield a landed price to the producer higher by the amount of the tariff presently paid to foreign governments or, alternatively, would be lowered in price to the foreign consumer so that more would be sold. Other firms, now unable to export because of foreign tariff or non-tariff protection, would find markets abroad. These firms would gain from greater volume of sales and might also reap dynamic gains from expanded production and economies of scale that would lower their unit costs. They would further benefit from the decline in the Canadian tariff, which would reduce their costs for equipment, supplies, and other inputs.

On the other hand, some Canadian firms would experience difficulties because of the removal of the Canadian tariff, since they have high prices and costs compared to the lowest-cost foreign sources of supply. Intensive competition from abroad would necessitate either a reorganization of production on more efficient lines or a contraction or even a disappearance if they were unable to achieve selling prices as low as those of imported goods.

Different responses can be envisaged for firms under pressure from increased foreign competition. One is a reorganization by firms to achieve specialization in fewer product lines and thus lower costs through a larger scale of production. Such reorganization would be possible in an international market because the elasticity of demand facing the firm would be greater than in the present constricted Canadian market for many manufactured goods. Moreover, when sales are made in a bigger market, the actions of each firm have fewer repercussions on its competitors and hence meet with less severe reductions in prices or other competitive response.

In other cases, firms would abandon some fields of production and apply their resources to more promising lines. Finally, a few firms would be unable to adjust and would close, thus releasing the factors of production that they were using to the expanding sectors of the economy, where these factors could be used more profitably.

All these adjustments would take time, involve losses to some firms and individuals and gains to others, and cause some temporary unemployment. Transitional policies would be designed to meet the special difficulties caused by the fundamental change in the structure of demand and the consequent necessity to adjust the structure of the Canadian economy.

Three logically distinct justifications exist for governmental intervention through transitional policies to aid those suffering losses as a consequence of a movement to free trade. The first is to provide compensation, from the public at large, for the injury suffered by some individuals in the process of change to a situation from which the whole society gains. The second is to assist those who suffer from the prospective change so that they will not effectively oppose a policy that will bring gains to society as a whole. The third, which recognizes the fact that markets function imperfectly and slowly, is to guide or hasten the reorganization of the economy so as to take advantage of the new opportunities brought by free trade.

The view that compensation should be given to individuals injured because the rules of the social and economic game are altered through a deliberate act of government depends on a conception of social justice. Full compensation would involve the payment to each import-competing firm of a sum equal to the difference betwen the price at which its products are sold with the tariff and the price it would have to meet without the tariff, multiplied by its sales. Such sums would, in theory, be paid not only to firms forced out of business by more intense international competition, but also to efficient firms that were still prospering under free trade. Both would have suffered from losses in the sense that the unit value of the sales of both firms would have declined, as compared with the position before free trade, and there seems to be no justification for giving compensation only to the failing firm, although this is usually the conception of people who speak of compensation.

Assisting those who would lose from a change in policy by "bribing" them, in effect, not to oppose the change has some abstract economic justification, in addition to being perhaps necessary as a political tactic to achieve policies that bring gains to society generally. Welfare economics teaches that if the gainers from a policy can compensate those who would lose from it, this is a proof that the policy in fact increases the welfare of society as a whole. Thus a successful bribe is an indication of social gain. However, it is unlikely that this process is a very good practical test in contemporary Canadian society, for two reasons. One is that losers are likely to be surer of, and more sensitive to, the extent of their potential losses than are gainers as to their potential gains. This is so because much of the gains would go to consumers, who are notoriously unorganized and incapable of defending their interests. (It is true, however, that export industries would also be gainers and that they would be conscious of their improved position.) The second difficulty with the practical application of the bribery test is that there are substantial costs involved in transfers from the gainers to the losers, these costs being the disincentive effects of imposing taxes on gainers and the administrative burden of making payments to the losers.

Intervention by the government to increase the effectiveness with which the market guides the factors of production from declining to expanding areas is the real and practical economic justification for transitional policies. The extent to which governmental intervention is necessary depends on the rigidity of the economy. An inflexible economy requires aid in combining factors of production in existing or new firms to produce the best collection of goods and services for the changed circumstances. Such aid could take the form of widespread training of managers and labour at public expense and of providing loans and grants for valid projects that private lenders could not recognize. On the other hand, a flexible economy managed by imaginative and adaptable people with access to capital might experience relatively little difficulty, so that the role of government in affording assistance would then be restricted to exceptional cases. Experience in the formation of the EEC and EFTA in Europe and in the administration of the Canada-U.S. automotive agreement on this continent indicates that the economies of advanced countries are, in fact, quite adaptable. In all these cases, much less has been required from government than had been expected.

A practical program for transitional policies might be quite complex, as was shown in the relevant study in the current series,[9] but its principal requirements are clear. The program should be oriented towards the anticipation of needs resulting from the institution of free trade and towards preparation for the changes that would be required, rather than to waiting and assessing the injury that resulted from free trade. The more effective such a program in providing incentives and aids to firms and workers in preparation for the changed situation, the smaller would be the actual injury to any of them.

The main provisions of such a program should relate, first, to safeguards in the trade agreement affecting the transitional period. Involved here would be the appropriate rate of changes in tariff protection in the transitional period and the special temporary treatment that might have to be given firms or plants in Canada relative to competitors already based in large markets abroad, especially the United States. Second, a battery of instruments to aid firms and individuals to adjust, through the provision of technical, managerial, marketing, labour-training, and financial support might be needed. Third, the weakest victims of the change might be given compensation.

One of the greatest problems in this connection concerns the separation of special adjustment devices in support of free trade from other welfare measures. Why should individuals and firms adversely affected by the institution of free trade be given privileged treatment relative to other firms in difficulty and individuals suffering from low incomes? Tying compensation to a particular cause would be justified only if the resources of government for aids to firms and individuals were limited relative to the need. In that case, tying such assistance to facilitate carrying out the single major policy change being attempted at the time—namely, the movement to free trade—might be expedient and wise. However, since it seems from experience and relevant analysis that fundamental difficulties caused by a major change in the conditions of international competition are likely to be remarkably rare, the need for support for individuals incapable of restoring their fortunes and firms unable to adjust to new situations may not be great. Therefore, the program for assistance in adjustment to economic change, developed for this purpose, might well be extended to all causes of dislocation and not only to those directly tied to amendments in Canadian tariff protection.

[9]Roy A. Matthews, *Industrial Viability in a Free Trade Economy: A Program of Adjustment Policies for Canada*, PPAC series "Canada in the Atlantic Economy," no. 12, Toronto, University of Toronto Press, 1971.

# 8. Some Commercial-Policy Conclusions[1]

## New challenges

This study on Canada and the Atlantic Economy was initiated about eight years ago, when it was realized that Canada's early postwar trade stance was no longer so appropriate in view of changing international circumstances. In particular, at that time the United States was fashioning a new policy in response to the reconstruction of Europe and the formation of the European Economic Community, which enabled—indeed, required—most of the countries of Western Europe to speak with a unified voice on trade matters. The course adopted was to initiate the Kennedy Round of trade negotiations under the General Agreement on Tariffs and Trade. What the Americans at first suggested was not only a further mutual reduction of tariffs along the lines of earlier rounds of negotiations, but also a special negotiation covering those categories of goods in which the EEC and the United States together constituted the "dominant" suppliers in world trade (80 percent or more of the total). This latter proposal presented an immediate challenge to Canada, since it forced this country to consider what economic role it should and could play in a world in which it might be neglected or downgraded in bargains between the large "Atlantic partners." This issue required answers to both economic and political questions: What would be the net benefit to Canada from alternative trade relationships? What would be the political consequences of closer integration in continental and world economies?

These questions remain important today (mid-1972), but some circumstances have altered, giving the issues a somewhat different character. The relevant changes since 1963 can be summarized as follows:

*First,* looking to Europe, Britain's membership in the European Com-

---

[1] As one of the authors of this volume, Bruce W. Wilkinson has a number of reservations about the conclusions of this chapter. Rather than attempting to spell them out here, he would refer the reader to Chapters 2 and 4 of this volume as well as to his article, "Recent American Tax Concessions to Industry and Canadian Economic Policy" (*Canadian Tax Journal,* 20, Jan.–Feb. 1972, esp. pp. 8–14), where several other issues are raised and some alternative suggestions are made.

munity, along with that of at least three other members of EFTA, seems, at long last, assured. While the longer-run effect of this upon trade with North America is not yet clear and cannot be until the EEC's common commercial policy has felt the influence of the new members, one thing is clear: Canada will no longer have any privileged position in the U.K. market. Henceforth Canadian access to British markets will be on the same basis as for other non-members of the EEC. Thus, Canadian exports will no longer enjoy the advantage of preferential Commonwealth rates, but will instead have to compete with shipments from EEC members that will be entering Britain duty-free.

Canada's situation is further weakened to the extent that new members of the EEC, or of the free trade association attached to the EEC to accommodate those EFTA partners who will not become full members (Sweden, Switzerland, Portugal, and Austria), have freer access to the EEC for products in which Canada has a comparative advantage, notably industrial materials. Because of this factor and the highly restrictive trade implications of the common agricultural policy, Canada's position as a supplier to Europe is weaker than that of the United States, for which finished manufactures are relatively more important.

*Second*, the spectacular growth of Japan during the 1960s has made that country the world's third-ranking industrial power. The relationship of Japan to its trading partners has taken on a growing importance, both economic and political. Both the United States and Western Europe have reacted more with fear than with imagination to the prospect of Japanese economic might. So far, no one has devised a means of effectively integrating Japan into the world economy. Part of the reason for the difficulty has been Japan's own protectionism in the form of traditional tariffs, price supports for agriculture, restrictions on foreign investment, and its somewhat mysterious administrative controls. But the retreat by Western countries into various forms of discrimination against Japanese goods, including devices such as voluntary export restraints, has provided no long-term solution. The opportunities for trade not only in Japan but in other expanding economies of the East make this aspect of Western economic policy much more important than it appeared to be less than a decade ago. The disarray of U.S. policy in Southeast Asia and recent U.S. overtures to China raise further the probable importance of trade and other economic policies relating to this region.

*Third*, the shift in U.S. attitudes since 1963 is likely to have the most pronounced effect on Canadian policy. Following the Kennedy Round, with its moderate success, the U.S. administration settled into a period of inactivity in the trade-policy area on the convenient excuse that it was necessary or desirable to allow time for the agreement to be fully implemented and the results to be observed. The reopening of negotiations between Britain and the EEC ensured that Europe would not be interested in serious trade negotiations for some time. Meanwhile, the disillusionment of U.S. public opinion with other aspects of the nation's international policies has reduced support for outward-looking policies. However, this was reflected in the U.S. administration only relatively recently, when the international monetary situation became intolerable. For many years, the growing U.S. balance of payments difficulties were treated with temporizing policies—mainly efforts to improve the liquidity of the international system or to control the outflow of U.S. capital. More fundamental adjustments were postponed for various reasons. American monetary specialists were reluctant to admit that the U.S. dollar was overvalued, using special effects of the Vietnam war as their explanation of current imbalances. But even when most U.S. authorities had come to accept the need for a shift in currency values, they were faced by the virtual impossibility of achieving this end, as a result of the reluctance of Europeans and Japanese to revalue. Finally, the tough position taken by the Nixon administration on August 15, 1971, did result in an important realignment of currencies.

Unfortunately, the August 15 measures also shook the confidence of supporters of liberal trade policy in the countries concerned. This was the consequence of the U.S. administration's rather clumsy attempts to tie the removal of the surcharge not only to currency realignment but also to national protective policies. Other countries were not willing to admit the relevance of their trade policies to the currency question or to acknowledge that the United States had fewer trade barriers (tariff and non-tariff) with which to bargain, quite apart from the surcharge. Because the exchange-rate settlement, albeit an interim one, was achieved—and achieved quite quickly—trade policy has now been restored to the pre-August 15 position. However, the U.S. administration is not in as strong a position as before when it comes to positive initiatives in trade policy. This applies particularly in 1972—a presidential election year—but it also has deeper political ramifications. The strong protectionist elements, especially now in the labour movement, are unlikely to be interested in liberalization of U.S. trade policies and can quote administration statements of recent months against any new move in that direction.

### Canada's inadequate responses

In a period of inertia and increasing difficulty with liberal trade policies, what has been Canada's position and how are new initiatives likely to be treated in these circumstances? The Canadian position has been responsive and not without occasional innovations (e.g., the auto pact), but it has generally been unsystematic and, above all, cautious to a fault. The first mistake was, of course, not to have pressed the United States for a more meaningful Kennedy Round. Had Canada sought a wider definition of the dominant supplier authority to include Britain and perhaps other EFTA countries and Canada itself, the Kennedy Round might have provided considerably greater scope for trade liberalization through the elimination of barriers on important categories of products.[2] It is important to recall that the U.S. Congress did broaden the negotiating authority, but that the administration urged Congress to withdraw the amendment in the hope that the narrower definition (to include the EEC but no other European countries in the dominant supplier group) might help to hasten Britain's acceptance as a member. Had Canada been active in putting pressure on the United States, the U.S. administration's error might have been avoided. However, at the time (the fall of 1962) Canada's political leaders were not on very good terms with the U.S. government and so missed an opportunity to influence it in a direction that could have been of considerable value to Canada.

The subsequent Kennedy Round made it clear how much Canada may have lost by failing to take advantage of the opportunity in 1962. Canadian spokesmen on trade policy argued that Canada could not go along with the United States, the EEC, and others in 50 percent tariff cuts because such cuts would expose Canadian industry to more severe new import competition. In other countries, it was argued, these tariff cuts would not affect international competitive positions so greatly because their industries were not so dependent upon such protection. If Canadian industries were to become less dependent upon protection, they would have to become more specialized and reliant on exports of certain lines. This could not be achieved, however, so long as *Canadian* tariffs encouraged firms to rely on diversified product patterns and *foreign* tariffs had to be absorbed in the cost of specialized exports. Basically, the point was that Canadian industry would regard it as worthwhile to restructure only if it could go the whole way and be put on really equal terms in international competition. The argument had some validity. The Kennedy Round approach (once the "dominant supplier" authority was side-tracked) was better suited to the larger trading units. But the outcome was not really satisfactory for Canada. Canada avoided reductions comparable to those granted by the United States and the EEC and ended up with one of the highest tariff schedules among developed

---

[2]See Howard S. Piquet, *The U.S. Trade Expansion Act of 1962* (Montreal and Washington, Canadian-American Committee, 1963), for an assessment of the scope for tariff elimination provided under the Trade Expansion Act.

countries. This means that Canada now has bargaining chips but no partners very interested in bargaining.

In retrospect, Canada appears to have treated trade policy from the viewpoint of the national negotiator who regards every tariff reduction as a cost (rather than a benefit to the consumer) and every unrequited reduction of other nations' trade barriers as a gain. In fact, all recent analysis of protected Canadian industries indicates that Canada's trade barriers have been at least as much responsible as foreign barriers for handicapping the development of efficient and internationally competitive production. What has been needed for some time is an approach to trade policy that is fully incorporated into industrial development strategy. Part of the problem is certainly the segregation in the Canadian public service of responsibility for tariffs and other trade barriers from responsibility for other aspects of industrial strategy.

But the main problem is the lack of priority afforded to this issue by Canada's political leaders. Successive cabinets seem to have been content to review and expand individual department policy programs rather than to attempt the sort of coordinated effort that might well economize on all their efforts. The federal government has a wide variety of industry and regional incentives and tax policies, a competition policy, and now even a separate cabinet assignment to deal with foreign investment, none of which are adequately coordinated with the others.

Possibly the main deterrent to a more coordinated approach is the lurking suspicion that it might require a fairly fundamental change in our conventional wisdom on trade policy—a change requiring acceptance of complete removal of trade barriers, and probably on a less than fully multilateral basis. This is intellectually resisted on several grounds. First, it is out of keeping with twenty-five years of commitment to GATT's so-called principles of non-discrimination. In fact, the GATT also permits, under Article 24, a regional approach to the multilateral objective, an approach that may be more appropriate to future negotiations in any case. Thus, it is probably to a second element in the Canadian conventional wisdom that one must look for the real source of failure of federal governments to devise a coherent industrial strategy. This is the fear of contemplating any regional scheme involving free trade with the United States. It is now commonplace for cabinet ministers to pass off such proposals by conjuring up fears of loss of independence. Yet there is nothing in the literature on trade that gives any logical basis for such a fear. If the will to political integration is lacking, does a nation give up its independence? Even in Western Europe, where many sought to extend a customs union or common market into some kind of federation, this has not occurred. Far from generating an inevitable evolutionary progress towards political integration, the EEC members appear in no great hurry to move beyond a partial market, apparently because most of the benefits of integration are being achieved and added benefits of closer economic ties are inadequate to warrant giving up national political prerogatives.

Canada should be able to make a choice of trade policies along with complementary industrial development initiatives in the light of its fundamental social interests, without becoming substantially more politically integrated with its trading partners.

The current trade-policy options for Canada have not really changed greatly over the years, and especially not since the end of the Kennedy Round. All that has really changed on the purely economic side is the clearer direction of European policy and the greater importance of the Pacific area. The most important options in this context are the following:

(a) the exploration and negotiation of non-tariff barriers under GATT auspices, and perhaps a further round of multilateral tariff reductions;

(b) the definition and negotiation of a Canada-U.S. free trade association;

(c) an application to become associated with the enlarged European Economic Community on terms comparable to those offered to Sweden and other European countries that do not wish full membership (an eventual free trade association including the EEC and these countries seems likely); and

(d) trade initiatives involving Japan.

## The traditional multilateral option

GATT is active in the study of non-tariff barriers. It seems likely that out of this study will emerge new rules governing some of the more familiar non-tariff practices that obstruct trade—e.g., valuation and classification practices and, perhaps, the more general quotas. The main difficulty with the handling of non-tariff barriers on a multilateral basis is the catch-all character of the category. The variety of these barriers increases the difficulty of distinguishing those that are minor irritants from those that have a significant contracting effect upon international trade. It is by no means clear that an effective code for dealing with the most general practices should really be given the highest priority. Some of the most trade-restricting practices are specific to certain national economies and deeply imbedded in long-standing domestic practices and institutions—for example, the agricultural policies of the EEC (and others), the purchasing policies of federal and state governments in the United States, and the "administrative" trade controls of Japan. Perhaps agricultural policies will be susceptible to multilateral negotiations, though the national packages of concessions required to achieve a rational pattern of international trade in such products are not of comparable size. If the effect on trade liberalization must be balanced, then the scope of concessions in agriculture will be determined by the modest package that less restrictive countries such as Canada can offer. What seems more likely is the sort of limited bilateral exchange of packages of non-tariff restrictions that has been under consideration since the early months of 1972 in the wake of the new exchange-rate settlement.

There is also the possibility of a new general tariff agreement. U.S. advisors to the President have recently proposed elimination of remaining tariffs among developed countries by the 1980s. This multilateral approach has an attractive simplicity to it until one asks two questions: (i) Would it apply to all products? (ii) How would it relate to non-tariff barriers? There is a very real prospect that such a proposal would apply only to industrial materials and manufactured products, that agricultural products would be left for separate negotiation, and that non-tariff barriers would be handled in the manner outlined above, leaving aside many trade-reducing practices. The most interesting possibility in any new GATT negotiation is that all countries might agree on the elimination of tariff barriers for intermediate goods and would retain lower and nationally uniform levels of tariffs on final products. This would greatly reduce the protected sector of the economy and would remove a substantial part of the structural distortion effects of the tariff. Only industries contributing a very small value added would enjoy continued high levels of effective protection, but the absolute advantage this would provide such industries should be small relative to the international market advantages enjoyed by industries based on distinctive Canadian resources or technological and other skills. The latter should command an even larger share of factor supplies than they do now.

Once distortions are reduced to the unavoidable minimum associated with national policy for protection of consumer goods manufacturers, it would be of relatively small significance for each country to have the same uniform rate on consumer products, because the exchange position or the relative rate of inflation would eventually reflect the differential levels of national protectionism. The main negotiating advantage of this situation is that different trading partners have important differences in their post-Kennedy Round tariffs. It would be easier to pay tribute to the traditional objective of equivalent concessions if, for example, GATT were to aim for something like the following levels: (i) for the United States and the EEC—not more than 5 percent; (ii) for Japan—not more than 7½ to 10 percent; and (iii) for smaller countries not attached to an industrial free trade group—not more than 12½ percent. But it would be important to get a commitment that the limit be uniform for each country or customs union, thus forestalling as many as possible of the subsequent complaints concerning discrimination against particular products regarded as having a comparative advantage by one of the trading partners.

One main difficulty with this approach is that it would require virtual free trade not only in many industrial materials that are already essentially freely traded, but also in such products as aluminum ingots, primary iron and steel up to the rolled-products level (at least), and industrial machinery and equipment. Negotiation on these product classes might be protracted, to say the least.

Another major difficulty, of course, is that those countries that rely on non-tariff barriers would be subject to heightened criticism from other trading partners when and if it became even more apparent that the trade-inducing effects of virtual elimination of tariffs were being thwarted by the non-tariff controls of these countries. The need for very specific commitments by the particular trading partners involved would then become urgent.

### The free-trade-group option

One of the advantages of a free trade association embodied in a formal treaty is that it commits all partners to the principle that subsequent national policy should not be allowed to frustrate the achievement of a pattern of trade and productive activity compatible with the free trade objective. Furthermore, it gives each partner a bargaining lever against policies that are not compatible with the spirit of the agreement. In any case, while it may be expected that multilateral efforts to reduce and control non-tariff barriers will continue for some time, it seems likely that trade-restricting effects of major national policies will challenge trading nations to devise new methods or new adaptations of old methods for achieving mutually acceptable liberalization.

The regional trade liberalization approach has many variants. For Canada, the main options are

(a) a Canada-U.S. grouping with some Latin American participation;

(b) a North Atlantic grouping with the EEC associated as a unit in a larger, looser grouping including members of EFTA who have not joined the EEC as full members, and perhaps the United States;

(c) a Pacific area group including Japan, Australia, and New Zealand as full members, and perhaps the United States.

These three options may be treated in a sense as substitutes or as complementary. By definition, any member of one free trade association may also be a member of others, since a common commercial policy vis-à-vis non-members is not required.[3] Nor are the complexities of such an inter-locking arrangement particularly serious as long as a system of certificates of origin can be used to keep track of imports entering a low-tariff member state.

On economic grounds, there is no longer much doubt that Canada's main benefits from further international integration would be derived from a Canada-U.S. arrangement, preferably one permitting a virtually free flow of agricultural products as well as of industrial materials and manufactures. Any arrangement that excluded the United States would severely handicap efforts of Canadian manufacturers to become effective in penetrating over-seas markets—their ability to achieve economies of scale in production and selling activities would then depend on more distant and less familiar markets. The area of the United States bordering Canada's industrial heartland offers the best opportunities for developing supply units of adequate scale for virtually every kind of manufacture Canada is likely to want to offer. Put another way, trade with overseas markets has always been concentrated more heavily in agricultural and industrial materials. The improvement in the relative role of exports of more advanced manufactures would be slower, probably much slower, if Canada depended primarily on overseas markets.

There are two main advantages in attempting to combine overseas arrange-ments with a deal involving the United States:

(1) the political value of having other close trading partners besides the United States; and

(2) the economic importance of keeping open, or re-opening, overseas markets for important Canadian agricultural and industrial materials.

The political factor is clearly very important in Canada. Probably no Canada-U.S. arrangement would be acceptable in Canada if another, similar arrangement with Europe or perhaps the Pacific countries were not also feasible. It would be politically difficult for any Canadian government to place high priority on measures leading to further economic integration in North America. It appears to be of little political significance that such measures, particularly those that concern only trade agreements, would not make a critical difference in the degree of interdependence of Canada and the United States.[4] The real reason for expanding trade relations overseas

[3]Britain and Ireland have had a free trade association while Britain was also a member of EFTA.

[4]No economist is prepared to argue that the proportion of Canada's trade that involves the United States (65 to 70 percent of both exports and imports) would change signifi-cantly if all formal trade barriers were removed in North America. Even if 80 percent of Canada's trade were with the United States, how would this affect the degree of political interdependence of the two nations?

in step with Canada-U.S. relations is that markets in the European Economic Community and the Far East are larger and fast-growing and that our ability to penetrate such markets should be substantially enhanced by the structural reorganization and the consequently improved efficiency made possible by freer trade on the North American continent.

The crucial question, as implied before, is whether a multilateral or a regional approach would be the preferable means of achieving the trade-liberalization objective. For reasons already cited, it is doubtful whether the multilateral approach will be effective, particularly in dealing with non-tariff policies. The success of a GATT Article 24 approach depends on Canadian will, particularly in respect of the Canada-U.S. arrangement, since it is very probable that the United States would accept a Canada-U.S. free trade association.[5] It is more uncertain whether the Europeans could permit any non-European participant in the proposed free trade association between the EEC and the non-Communist countries of Europe that remain uninterested or ineligible for full membership in the EEC. It seems unlikely that any serious thought has been given in the EEC to Canadian participation in a European-based free trade group. If Canada raised such an issue, the European countries would be concerned about setting a precedent by accepting any non-European member. Still, if they are serious about a new initiative towards trade liberalization, the expansion of a European-based free trade association might well have special appeal to the Europeans. But it must be remembered that Canada would not be entirely satisfied with any basis of association with the EEC that failed to provide some scope for increasing Canadian agricultural exports.

It should be added that if this sort of arrangement were sought by Canada alone, without the United States, the latter might well adopt very tough bargaining positions vis-à-vis Canada, though this would not likely be related explicitly by Washington to any Canadian initiative towards the EEC. Of course, Canada could avoid this problem by parallel or independent negotiations with Washington. The problem would be more serious if, as some Canadians appear to wish, the Canadian government were deliberately to attempt an Atlantic initiative as a way of diverting its trade from the United States.

The prospect of a Pacific initiative rests with Japan. While there has been some talk in Japan of a Pacific free trade area, it may be that this represents a characteristic probing of all longer-term options rather than any firm indi-

[5]Since the dispute over the auto pact and the Connally incident, American negotiators would certainly take a tougher stand in their dealings with Canada, but this does not mean that a free trade association is unacceptable. In fact, even the toughest U.S. negotiators have hinted that it is precisely a comprehensive "deal" with Canada that they would find most acceptable.

cation of government intent. According to Japanese observers, the government and industry are moving towards a reappraisal of traditional protectionism. They now realize the cost-raising effects of their agricultural policies and the need to accept more agricultural products from trading partners in the Pacific if their own exports of manufactures are to have improved access to such markets. They also recognize the need for some modification of administrative practices and (or) foreign investment controls so that their manufacturing trade will not be repeatedly subjected to new non-tariff barriers, especially by North American trading partners. Whether it would be possible to design a free trade association in the Pacific remains uncertain, but Japan appears to be increasingly motivated in this direction. At any rate, there is no doubt that it is in Canada's interest to encourage trade liberalization by Japan, and specifically to seek package agreements covering non-tariff as well as tariff factors. Such packages could conceivably work to both countries' advantage in dealings with the United States.

One of the most important arguments for any of these regional groups is that they could be important means of reaching a consistent policy towards trade with the developing countries. The simplest formula would be for each free trade association to give unilateral free access to members' markets for the exports of related developing countries. Just as the EEC now gives limited free access to the products of Africa, so Canada and the United States might afford similar access to Latin American goods, and the Pacific developed countries might give leadership in the same direction on behalf of Asian products.

The aim of all such efforts through regional arrangements is to work towards multilateral liberalization of remaining tariffs and to limit the scope of existing—and possible future—non-tariff barriers, including those deeply embedded in national policies.

### Canadian national aims and industrial development strategy

The central questions in Canada in the early 1970s concern priorities that will govern Canada's foreign relations and the importance that trade-policy initiatives will have in the pursuit of these priorities. The statement of Canadian foreign-policy aims contained in the foreign-policy review, *Foreign Policy for Canadians*,[6] gives much recognition to economic aims. Among those singled out are (1) to foster economic growth; (2) to promote social justice; (3) to enhance the quality of life. The other three stated objectives (safeguarding of sovereignty and independence, working for peace and

[6]Department of External Affairs, *Foreign Policy for Canadians*, Ottawa, Queen's Printer, 1970.

security, and ensuring a harmonious natural environment) have been somewhat downgraded in Canadian policy debates, basically on the grounds that the Cold War détente and the recovery of Europe have reduced Canada's role as a factor in international security and have reduced its main concerns to the fields of trade, investment, and aid, with a corresponding increased interest in the other continents.

But the question that was avoided by the foreign-policy review was the role of Canadian-American relations in Canada's pursuit of national aims.[7] As already indicated in this chapter, it would appear to be an essential role, particularly in relation to the aim of economic growth. But many doubts are raised nowadays about the importance of growth, and, indeed, there appears to be conflict in the eyes of some between an emphasis upon quality of life and social justice, as somehow more appropriate goals for Canada, on the one hand, and an emphasis upon economic growth, which is often represented as more characteristic of the United States, on the other. In fact, much of this conflict arises out of the vagueness of the expressions used. Economic growth does encompass two rather different processes, increased output due to greater efficiency and the enlargement of productive capacity due to higher levels of investment, whether it be in the form of expanded factories, newly explored natural resources, new skills imparted to the labour force, or improved technology. The latter processes do involve shifting resources away from the supply of current consumption needs. In a priority system that defines the improved quality of life in terms of a richer and more balanced mix of public and private goods and services, higher levels of private investment may have less relative merit. Improved efficiency, however, involves no such problem of sacrificing current consumption, since the resulting expansion of production can be devoted to enlarging either consumption or investment activity, in line with national social preferences.

Since international competitiveness will promote greater efficiency and, indeed, is one of the most effective forces towards this end, it seems that this kind of objective can be pursued without hesitation.

Whether because the foregoing distinction is not well understood or for some other reason, it does not appear that Canadian public policy is headed in the near future in the direction of any substantial new move towards trade liberalization. Apparently, for many the fear of trade competition goes hand in hand with distaste for American investment, and because of the desire

[7]This omission has been remedied by a recent article prepared by the staff of the Department of External Affairs, "Canada-U.S. Relations: Options for the Future" (*International Perspectives*, Autumn 1972). The article is mainly a reiteration of conventional fears concerning U.S. dominance and concludes with a touching faith in government intervention as a substitute for trade liberalization in meeting the challenge of international competition.

somehow to limit the role of foreign ownership of Canadian resources and industries, many are willing to forgo the benefits of access to the large U.S. market and the invigorating influence of exposure to U.S. competition. In Canada the will to succeed in international competition is not very strong, and the confidence to negotiate adequate commercial arrangements, including appropriate adjustment provision for the transition period, appears to be lacking.

Canadian governments seem most likely to rely on a package of domestic policies intended to constitute a kind of industrial development program. Clearly this will include some sort of competition policy, measures relating to the encouragement of domestic ownership and control of Canadian industry, and various tax and subsidy arrangements to encourage Canadian industrial development.

But such policies, while having considerable merit (if only because international competition cannot be a guarantor of the efficiency of all markets), are likely to have less clarity of purpose in the absence of the discipline of international competition. Competition policy may have to be more interventionist in domestic markets that are clearly isolated from international competitive forces, and there may be much more pressure for direct control of industry. More direct foreign-investment controls may have to be employed to correct the inefficiencies the Canadian protective system preserves in many externally controlled manufacturing industries. Tax-credit and other incentive "carrots" will not be accompanied by the "stick" of international competition. None of these policies need be ineffective, but all will probably be more interventionist in the absence of the best source of market discipline available in the modern mixed economy. For a country of Canada's size and with Canada's structural problems, industrial development strategy without a very liberal foreign trade policy seems like "Hamlet without the prince."

But it is not only industrial development strategy that is at stake. Canada's efforts to resolve the unemployment problem without substantial price inflation and its ability to expand real development opportunities in the outlying regions of Canada can both be enhanced by liberal trade policies— the former because upward price and wage pressures are better resisted as unemployment declines if competitive forces are stronger, the latter because the scope for expanding industrial activity in the Maritimes and British Columbia is certain to be enhanced by providing these areas with access to markets in the United States that are much closer to them and much larger than the central Canadian market. Without such access, these regions will have to depend almost exclusively upon resource-based activities for some time to come.

# RELATED PUBLICATIONS BY THE
# PRIVATE PLANNING ASSOCIATION OF CANADA

## THE WORLD ECONOMY

*The World Economy at the Crossroads: A Survey of Current Problems of Money, Trade and Economic Development*, by Harry G. Johnson, 1965.

*The International Monetary System: Conflict and Reform*, by Robert A. Mundell, 1965.

## CANADA'S TRADE RELATIONSHIPS

*Canada and Latin America: The Potential for Partnership*, by Colin I. Bradford, Jr., and Caroline Pestieau, 1972.

*Japan: Challenge and Opportunity for Canadian Industry*, by Keith Hay, 1971.

*China's External Trade – A Canadian Perspective*, by Claude E. Forget, 1971.

*Canada's Trade Policy in the Second Development Decade*, by Benjamin and Jean Higgins, 1970.

*Canada's International Trade: An Analysis of Recent Trends and Patterns*, by Bruce Wilkinson, 1968.

*Canada's Trade with the Communist Countries of Eastern Europe*, by Ian M. Drummond, 1966.

*Canada's Role in Britain's Trade*, by Edward M. Cape, 1965.

*The Common Agricultural Policy of the E.E.C. and Its Implications for Canada's Exports*, by Sol Sinclair, 1964.

*Canada's Interest in the Trade Problems of Less-Developed Countries*, by Grant L. Reuber, 1964.

## CANADA'S COMMERCIAL POLICY AND COMPETITIVE POSITION

*Non-Tariff Trade Barriers As a Problem in International Development*, by Caroline Pestieau and Jacques Henry, 1972.

*Prices, Productivity, and Canada's Competitive Position*, by N. H. Lithwick, 1967.

## CANADA-U.S. ECONOMIC RELATIONS

*The New Environment for Canadian-American Relations*, a Statement by the Committee, 1972.

*Canada's Experience with Fixed and Flexible Exchange Rates in a North American Capital Market*, by Robert M. Dunn, Jr., 1971.

*Toward a More Realistic Appraisal of the Automotive Agreement*, a Statement by the Committee, 1970.

*The Canada-U.S. Automotive Agreement: An Evaluation*, by Carl E. Beigie, 1970.

*North American Agriculture in a New World*, by J. Price Gittinger, 1970.

*The Performance of Foreign-Owned Firms in Canada*, by A. E. Safarian, 1969.

*Constructive Alternatives to Proposals for U.S. Import Quotas* (a Statement by the Committee), 1968.

*U.S.-Canadian Free Trade: The Potential Impact on the Canadian Economy*, by Paul Wonnacott and Ronald J. Wonnacott, 1968.

*The Role of International Unionism in Canada,* by John H. G. Crispo, 1967.

*A New Trade Strategy for Canada and the United States* (a Statement by the Committee), 1966.

*Capital Flows between Canada and the United States,* by Irving Brecher, 1965.

*A Possible Plan for a Canada-U.S. Free Trade Area* (a Staff Report), 1965.

FORTHCOMING

*Canadian Non-Tariff Barriers to Trade,* by Klaus F. Stegemann with appendices by Caroline Pestieau.

*The Development of the Canadian Anti-Dumping System,* by Rodney de C. Grey.